EPHESIANS
The Unsearchable Riches of Christ

Roy W. Hefti

A Devotional Commentary

NORTHWESTERN PUBLISHING HOUSE
Milwaukee, Wisconsin

Cover: Image used under extended license from Lightstock
Design: Amy Malo

Scripture quotations are from the Holy Bible, Evangelical Heritage Version® (EHV®) ©2019 Wartburg Project, Inc. All rights reserved. Used by permission.

Hymn references marked CW are from *Christian Worship: Hymnal* © 2021 by Northwestern Publishing House.

All rights reserved. This publication may not be copied, photocopied, reproduced, translated, or converted to any electronic or machine-readable form in whole or in part, except for brief quotations, without prior written approval from the publisher.

Northwestern Publishing House
N16W23379 Stone Ridge Dr., Waukesha WI 53188-1108
www.nph.net
© 2025 by Northwestern Publishing House
Published 2025
Printed in the United States of America
ISBN 978-0-8100-3306-1
ISBN 978-0-8100-3307-8 (e-book)

To all my children

Introduction

The epistles of the New Testament are indeed letters, but they are letters written by inspiration of the Holy Spirit, letters written to certain Christians and congregations under certain circumstances. In these instances, God actually wants us to read someone else's mail . . . because these letters are written for us too.

Paul perhaps has a chain dangling from his wrist as he writes this letter, one end attached to him and the other to a Roman soldier (Ephesians 6:20; Acts 28:20). Paul is under house arrest in Rome, awaiting his turn to stand trial before Caesar. His ministry is not entirely over. He will eventually be released to preach again, perhaps getting as far as Spain with the gospel. Then his second imprisonment will come, when the door of the dungeon will swing open and he will go forth to execution. From that cold dungeon he will write one last letter to Timothy, saying, "The time of my departure has come. I have fought the good fight; I have finished the race; I have kept the faith" (2 Timothy 4:6-7).

But even here in his first imprisonment, more of life is behind him than ahead of him. The shadows are lengthening for the lion of God in winter. Time hangs heavy on his hands. He writes to a few of the congregations he founded. You and I know these as the letters to the Ephesians, Philippians, Colossians, and Philemon.

The folks in Ephesus are old friends. Paul had spent three years among them during his third missionary journey (Acts 19–20). Acts chapter 20 gives us the backstory of the last time he saw them. Paul gathers the pastors of Ephesus on the beach at Miletus to say farewell. His words are punctuated by the ebb and flow of the splashing tide. He cared for the people to whom he preached. It broke his heart whenever some rejected the Word. It thrilled him when they believed. Publicly and personally, he preached the same message: They must turn to God in repentance and have faith in the Lord Jesus. They must believe God when he tells them about their sin. And they must believe God when he tells them their sins are forgiven. There is no greater dishonor to God than not to believe him—to remain in our sins or to despair of the forgiveness that the Lord Jesus Christ died and rose to give us.

Paul sums up his ministry among the Ephesians by saying, "I did not hesitate to proclaim to you the whole counsel of God" (Acts 20:27). Law and gospel, sin and grace, bitter and sweet— Paul preached *God's* Word, not his own. The Savior said, "Watch out for false prophets. They come to you in sheep's clothing, but inwardly they are ravenous wolves" (Matthew 7:15). Paul sounds a similar warning: "Always keep watch over yourselves and over the whole flock in which the Holy Spirit has placed you as overseers, to shepherd the church of God, which he purchased with his own blood. I know that after my departure savage wolves, who will not spare the flock, will come in among you. Even from your own group men will rise up, twisting the truth in order to draw away disciples after them. Therefore be always on the alert!" (Acts 20:28-31). Knowing that no preacher can forever ensure the orthodoxy of the generations that follow, Paul does the only thing he can. He says, "Now I entrust you to God and to the word of his grace" (20:32).

These are the people and this is the backstory of this little letter to the Christians at Ephesus. Keying off of sermons preached in 2013 at St. Paul's Evangelical Lutheran Church in

Bangor, Wisconsin, this commentary aims to be devotional, practical, and plain to the average reader, while being mindful of the Greek text behind the English translation (EHV).

Unlike Paul's letter to the Galatians, this letter does not reference a specific crisis or controversy plaguing the believers in Ephesus. Instead, the themes of this letter to the Ephesians are wide-ranging. They are high and deep, long and wide. Paul sets forth *the unsearchable riches of Christ* to bless the church of all ages until the Savior comes again. By faith, these riches belong to you and me too.

Pastor Roy W. Hefti

EPHESIANS
The Unsearchable Riches of Christ

Contents

	Introduction	v
1:1-14	The Plan	1
1:15-23	A Pastor's Prayer	9
2:1-10	Dead or Alive	17
2:11-22	All in the Family	27
3:1-13	The Secret Is Out!	35
3:14-21	Infinitely More!	47
4:1-16	Family Ties	55
4:17-32	Get a Life!	65
5:1-21	How Shall We Then Live?	73
5:22-33	The Mystery of Christ's Love for Us Inspires Our Own	81
6:1-4	The Spirit Turns Our Hearts Toward Home	89
6:5-9	Being Filled With the Spirit Sets Our Hearts Free	97
6:10-17	Put On the Full Armor of God!	107
6:18-24	Pray!	115

EPHESIANS

1:1-14
The Plan

Is there a plan? Or is there no plan? Is life just random? Just one mindless thing after another? One person lives to be 9; another lives to be 90. One person hits every possible pothole in the road; another cruises down the highway with barely a speed bump. One toils 12 hours a day for minimum wage; another hardly breaks a sweat and lives in luxury.

Is there a plan? Not just for nations and empires and not just for the rich and famous but for all the separate souls, for the poor and nameless? For you and for me and for the weary faces wandering up and down the aisles of Walmart or trudging through airport terminals? Is there a plan? The Bible says there is. But that would imply that someone is doing the planning, wouldn't it? Someone is. Paul says so . . . here on the front porch of his letter to the Ephesians. The plan is God's plan. Lifelong Christians have often heard it called the plan of salvation. The plan was made *before* time. It came to pass *in* time. It comes to pass for us *on* time.

So let's open Paul's letter to the Ephesians and see what he has to say.

> **¹Paul, an apostle of Christ Jesus by the will of God, To the saints who are in Ephesus, who are believers in Christ Jesus: ²Grace to you and peace from God our Father and the Lord Jesus Christ.**

Paul shows us his credentials. He is "an apostle of Christ Jesus by the will of God." The words he writes are not his words but God's words.

The first folks to receive this letter are the "saints who are in Ephesus." We sing hymns that speak of saints: "For all the saints who from their labors rest." Our Communion liturgy reminds us that "all the saints on earth" join their voices with all the "hosts of heaven" in one mighty chorus of praise each Sunday (CW, p. 166). The word *saints* refers not to sinless people, nor to some select group of dead folks who will get us through to God's throne if we pray to them. The Bible uses the word *saints* to refer to believers in Christ. Sometimes we refer to prominent believers of the past with that word: Saint Paul, Saint John, etc. Yet all Christians, those at Ephesus as well as you and I, are saints—literally—people set apart; people around whom God has drawn a circle by faith in Jesus Christ as our only Savior. Here we are, inside the circle of God's love and friendship.

Paul perhaps has a chain attached to his wrist as he writes this letter. He writes from Rome during his first imprisonment, while under house arrest. Eventually, he will be released to preach again. Then during his second and last imprisonment, he will suffer the chill of the dungeon before going forth to execution. The folks in Ephesus are old friends. Paul spent three years there on his third missionary journey. It has been a few years now since Paul gathered the pastors of Ephesus on the beach at Miletus

1:1-14 The Plan

to say farewell, warning them to beware of false prophets—savage wolves.

Paul points them and us to the "grace . . . and peace" that come equally from God the Father and God the Son. To veterans of the faith, *grace* and *peace* can become shopworn, churchy words. It is easy to tune them out. But the Bible clothes the word *grace* with the flesh and bones of King David, who came forth from the pit of despair to breathe the sweet air of God's pardon after a one-night stand with another man's wife and the murderous cover-up when the pregnancy test came back positive. *Grace* is the returning prodigal son surprised by the bear hug of his father. *Grace* is a dying thief promised paradise. *Grace* is Paul himself, a former persecutor, called out of the night into the light to be Christ's apostle. *Grace* is you . . . me . . . finding out that Jesus planned to trade places with us before we were born.

And "peace . . ." *Peace* is the way things are supposed to be between God and us who have declared war on him. *Peace* is what Christ negotiated between us and our Father at the frightful cost of his own blood. *Peace* is Peter, sound asleep in the dungeon even when he knows Herod has scheduled his execution for the next day. Grace and peace are all part of the plan that God made *before* time, that came to pass *in* time, and that comes to pass for you and me *on* time. Here is God's plan for you and me, a plan formed *before* time existed.

> **³Blessed be the God and Father of our Lord Jesus Christ, who has blessed us in Christ with every spiritual blessing in the heavenly places. ⁴He did this when he chose us in Christ before the foundation of the world, so that we would be holy and blameless in his sight. In love ⁵he predestined us to be adopted as his sons through Jesus Christ. He did this in accordance with the good purpose of his will, ⁶and for the praise**

of his glorious grace, which he has graciously given us in the one he loves.

God's plan has always been to bless us with every spiritual blessing in Christ Jesus, never apart from Christ Jesus. God surely blesses us with food and drink, house and home, spouse and children, and all those other First Article blessings that sustain body and life in this world. But the blessings that count and the blessings that last are the Second and Third Article blessings, the good news of him who died and rose again and the Holy Spirit's gift of faith to make all this our own—spiritual blessings that flow from "the heavenly places."

The plan was made before time existed, "before the foundation of the world." It was in that timelessness of eternity that God chose us. Remember how often the people of Israel in the Old Testament were called God's "chosen people"? Why? Not because of their own righteousness, says the Lord in Deuteronomy (9:6), but simply because the Lord loved them. Or as Jesus put it: "You did not choose me, but I chose you" (John 15:16).

Here God lets believers see beneath the surface and behind the curtain of life. I am not an accidental blob of evolutionary goo. I am not one more nameless face in a herd of billions. God knew me and loved me before I was born. He looked at me through the bloody lens of his Son's sacrifice. In Christ, God chose me to be holy and blameless in his sight. He predestined me—determined ahead of time to adopt me as his son (a legal term regardless of gender) in the gospel waters of Baptism—to make me his legal heir, destined to inherit heaven itself. An inheritance is not something I have earned. It is by its very nature a gift, something that was earned for me by the life and labors of someone else. That someone else had to die before I could receive the inheritance. God's own Son did just that.

The plan came to pass *in* time:

1:1-14 The Plan

⁷In him we also have redemption through his blood, the forgiveness of sins, in keeping with the riches of his grace, ⁸which he lavished on us in all wisdom and insight.

When Martin Luther was a monk in the Augustinian cloister, he used to agonize over this doctrine of election: that God, out of pure love for the sake of Christ, chose specific souls from eternity to come to faith in time and to finally be saved. He worried: "What if I am not one of the elect?" Doctor Staupitz, sitting under the old pear tree, gave the young monk a piece of advice he never forgot: "Brother Martin, first find yourself in the wounds of Christ, and then you can be sure of your election" (as the writer recalls Dr. Siegbert Becker citing Luther). Years later Luther was reported to have remarked regarding Staupitz that beneath that cursed old monk's cowl beat a truly evangelical heart.

The plan unfailingly came to pass *in* time. The Bible says we have redemption through Christ's blood, the forgiveness of sins. We were held hostage by sin, death, and hell, and Christ paid the ransom of his own blood to buy us back. He did this not just for some. He did this for all. The Bible says that Christ is the Lamb of God who takes away the sin of the world. Jesus told Nicodemus, "God so loved the world that he gave his only-begotten Son" (John 3:16). Paul told the Corinthians, "God was in Christ reconciling the world to himself" (2 Corinthians 5:19). Are you part of the world? Of course. Then God's eternal plan includes you. God has written your name in Christ, who is the real book of life. Believe it.

This plan for you and me comes to pass *on* time:

⁹He made known to us the mystery of his will in keeping with his good purpose, which he planned in Christ. ¹⁰This was to be carried out when the time

> had fully come, in order to bring all things together in Christ, things in heaven and things on earth. **¹¹In him we have also obtained an inheritance, because we were predestined according to the plan of him who works out everything in keeping with the purpose of his will. ¹²He did this so that his glory would be praised as a result of us, who were the first to hope in Christ. ¹³In him, when you heard the word of truth, the gospel of your salvation, and in him, when you also believed, you were sealed with the promised Holy Spirit. ¹⁴He is the down payment of our inheritance until the redemption of God's own possession, so that his glory would be praised.**

The plan would do us little good if we did not know about it so that we could believe it. This mystery needs to be revealed, taught, and preached. That is how it comes to pass for all those who believe in Christ. The biblical doctrine of election, God's plan for you, is simply this: *Before* time was, God set his love on you out of pure grace. In Christ, he elected, or chose, you to be his very own. *In* time, God brought this to pass by sending his only begotten Son to redeem you by his life, death, and resurrection. *On* time, God the Holy Spirit brought you to faith through the gospel in Word and sacraments. He has promised to keep you in that faith all the way to heaven.

Do not spoil this comfort with questions that God has not answered. God did not give us this teaching about his eternal plan as an intellectual plaything, to probe why some and not others. He has not predestined the so-called others to damnation. The Bible speaks of "God our Savior, who wants all people to be saved and to come to the knowledge of the truth" (1 Timothy 2:3-4). People are lost not because of some monstrous, arbitrary decree of God but by their own stubborn unbelief. People are saved not because they were or would be nobler or smarter than the so-called others but because of God's amazing grace alone. Those who are the elect will be preserved to eternal life. This will become evident as they cross the finish line into eternity. Yet on this side of the grave, the Bible does not teach "once saved, always saved." If I am careless and secure in my sins, then I need to be reminded that King Saul, Judas, and many others lost the faith they once had. "Let him who thinks he stands be careful that he does not fall" (1 Corinthians 10:12) is the word of the law I then need to hear. But when I tremble at how many casualties lie strewn on the path around me, then I need to hear not one word of the law's finger-wagging threats. I need to hear only the gospel of Christ's promise, "No one will snatch them out of my hand" (John 10:28), and Paul's words, "He who began a good work in you will carry it on to completion" (Philippians 1:6). I must not seek to peek behind the curtain of things that God has declared are none of my business. I need only see my election, my place in God's plan, carved indelibly in the nail-pierced hands of my Savior.

The plan is for you and me too, for Jews and Gentiles alike. Paul says, "In him, when you heard the word of truth, the gospel of your salvation, and in him, when you also believed, you were sealed with the promised Holy Spirit. He is the down payment of our inheritance until the redemption of God's own possession, so that his glory would be praised." In bringing us to believe, we were marked as God's own by the indwelling of the Holy Spirit. The Holy Spirit himself is the deposit, the down payment, the guarantee of the payment in full that will surely be ours in heaven. This is the plan that presses from the lips of the saints on earth and all the hosts of heaven—an eternal hymn of praise for his amazing grace.

Is there a plan? Or is there no plan? Is life just random? Just one mindless thing after another? Now you and I know. Here Jesus draws us close and whispers in our ears a stunning secret, a mystery revealed only to those inside his circle by faith. Jesus says, "I know the storm is often loud and the wind is against you. I know your heart sometimes beats fast with fear. I know you struggle with sin in you and around you. But stay here with me inside the circle, and I will show you the whole plan and the last chapter too, the happy ending. I promise you, safe on the other side, we will celebrate together. It will be 'like spring after winter, and sun on the leaves; and like trumpets and harps and all the songs [you] have ever heard!' (J. R. R. Tolkien, *The Return of The King*). That's my plan for you, and I am sticking to it!"

EPHESIANS

1:15-23
A Pastor's Prayer

There's a story from 1529, a year before the Lutherans would present the Augsburg Confession to Emperor Charles V, spelling out grace alone, faith alone, and Scripture alone. Three Lutheran delegates journeyed to Italy to present their protest to the emperor. One of them, named Frauentraut, boldly told His Majesty that in the end they must answer to the Supreme Judge, not to creatures who turn at every wind, and that they would obey no decrees that were not founded on the Holy Scriptures. Charles V politely listened. Then he arrested all three and threw them in prison. A Lutheran prince named Philip of Hesse wrote a letter to Martin Luther asking the great reformer to help. He figured Luther could use his connections with the Prince of Saxony to work out a political solution to the problem.

Luther responded, "I will pray." You can just about imagine Philip's reaction to Luther's letter: "What? You will pray? That's the best get-out-of-jail-free card you've got to offer? Is that all you are going to do? Can't you do more?" Even pastors who hear this little episode might feel Luther's response is sort of inadequate, half-hearted, and disappointing.

Anyone acquainted with Luther knows that he didn't have his head in the clouds. He often found very practical ways to help people. But with our foot on the gas pedal and our hand on a smartphone, we have a hard time relating to a man who used to say that when he was having a very hard and busy day, he would have to spend an extra hour in prayer!

But the rest of the story? A few weeks later, the three imprisoned men somehow got hold of some horses in the middle of the night and galloped away at full speed along a road infested with soldiers and bandits. Did Luther couple his hours of prayer with a few winks and nods to friends who knew how to help? After five hundred years, Luther still isn't talking.

But Luther saw this thing called prayer as an important part of his ministry. He learned from the Scriptures, especially from Paul, that preaching, pastoring, and praying go together. Here in his letter to the Ephesians, Paul puts his heart in the display window with a pastor's prayer—a prayer of thanks for the faith we already have, a prayer that we may know God even better, a prayer that the eyes of our hearts may be enlightened.

As he so often does in his letters, Paul thanks God for the faith that the Christians at Ephesus already have:

> **[15]This is why, ever since I heard about your faith in the Lord Jesus and your love for all the saints, [16]I never stop giving thanks for you, remembering you in my prayers.**

It's probably been about five years since Paul spoke that tearful farewell to the folks at Ephesus, warning them to watch out for savage wolves—false teachers who would not spare the flock. Now, while under house arrest in Rome, the old apostle hears

1:15-23 A Pastor's Prayer

through his grapevine that the Ephesians are still strong in their faith and that false prophets have not yet made inroads into the congregation.

As we listen in on this pastor's prayer, we see that Paul has his priorities straight. Praise and thanks come first; petitions and requests come second. Paul knows more than most how easily praying can turn into whining. Persecuted and imprisoned, stoned and shipwrecked, betrayed by false brothers and embattled by false teachers, Paul could easily whine about the crosses and the losses he has shouldered.

But the losses and liabilities do not blind the apostle to the good stuff in his ministry. He sees it as a miracle that *anyone* should believe. Paul says to the believers in Ephesus: "I never stop giving thanks for you, remembering you in my prayers." Each of the congregations Paul has founded, as with multiple children in one family, has its own personality, its own strengths and weaknesses. Some of those congregations are more problematic than others. But as Paul so often does, when he thinks of the congregation in Ephesus, his first impulse is not to complain about the no-shows, cheapskates, fornicators, and foul mouths in the congregation, although the church at Ephesus probably has its share of them.

Rather, Paul's first impulse is to thank God for what the good news of Christ has already accomplished in the hearts of those to whom he pens this letter. He is grateful for the faith that is already in the Ephesians. Like pastors throughout the ages, he is amazed that souls who once had no appetite for the Bread of Life now can't get enough of it; that hearts once weighed down with idols that could not help them have found a Father who carries them; that minds once tortured with guilt have found in Christ the peace that passes understanding; and that despite the chorus of voices enticing them down a different path, they have remained true to the Word. A pastor need not look far to see the miracles worked by the gospel: Someone whose whole life is colored by one disaster after another still shows up each week with a smile. Someone who would never have darkened the doorstep of the church ten years ago now can't stay away. A young person whose parents and siblings care nothing for the Word of Life courageously shows up to sit in a pew alone. Someone who has eyes to see the downhearted leads a friend to Christ. For those who do show up, for those who do believe, for those who stay when others walk out, a pastor's prayer is this: "I never stop giving thanks for you, remembering you in my prayers."

Paul sees praying for the flock as a large part of the ministry. He prays that the people may know God even better:

[17]I keep praying that the God of our Lord Jesus Christ, the glorious Father, will give you the Spirit of wisdom and revelation in knowing Christ fully.

When President and Mrs. Kennedy wanted to make the White House a center of the arts and culture during the so-called days of Camelot, it was not surprising that one of the performers they invited to the White House was the great cellist Pablo Casals. When Pablo Casals was well into his nineties, a young reporter asked him why he still practiced for hours each day. Casals replied, "Because I think I'm making progress."

With a matter-of-fact prayer to the Trinity—the glorious Father, the Lord Jesus Christ, and the Spirit of wisdom and revelation—Paul's prayer is that God's people will know Christ fully. In a perfect world, our faith would always grow stronger and more mature. But in a world stunk up by the sin around us and in us, it is not automatic that you and I will love Christ more and know God's Word better when we are 90 than when we were 9. It is not automatic that a 40-year-old has a better understanding of Christian doctrine than a 14-year-old who has just finished

1:15-23 A Pastor's Prayer

confirmation instruction. Instinctively, little children desire to grow up, to learn more, to move from the car seat to the driver's seat and from being spoon-fed to feeding themselves. So why is it, when it comes to their life with God, their knowledge of the Scriptures, and their mature Christian behavior, many Christians are content to stay in spiritual Pampers and on a diet of spiritual Gerber's?

A pastor's prayer is that we may know God better. A thousand lifetimes are too little to fully taste God's menu. Perhaps, without sounding a trumpet about it or with little fanfare, you have noted something. The Holy Spirit has created in you a spiritual appetite. You find great joy in reading the Bible, in attending worship and Bible study, in reviewing your catechism, in making the hymnal your prayer book, in reading a *Meditations* booklet. Keep doing this. You will get to know God better. This growth is a tricky thing. Like a child growing from infancy to adulthood, sometimes there are growth spurts—easy to see. Sometimes

growth is slow, almost imperceptible. Only a person who has not seen the child for some time would be struck by the growth that has occurred. People who meet a tall young man for the first time have no idea what a runt he may have been. Many have grown over the years in their faith, in their love and knowledge of God, more than they themselves know—simply by regular, devout attention to Word and Sacrament. This is the work of the Spirit of wisdom and revelation for which Paul prays. There is no need for us to obsess over ourselves or take our own spiritual pulse every day any more than one would plant potatoes and then dig them up every day to see how they are doing. Let us simply trust that wherever we and the Word come together, we can say with old Pablo Casals, "I think I'm making progress."

Thankful for the faith the Ephesians already have and praying they may get to know God even better, Paul's pastoral prayer is that the eyes of their hearts may be enlightened to see just how blessed they are:

> **[18] I pray that the eyes of your heart may be enlightened, so that you may know the hope to which he has called you, just how rich his glorious inheritance among the saints is, [19] and just how surpassingly great his power is for us who believe. [20] It is as great as the working of his mighty strength, which God worked in Christ when he raised him from the dead and seated him at his right hand in the heavenly places, [21] far above all rule, authority, power, and dominion, and above every name that is given, not only in this age but also in the one to come. [22] God also placed all things under his feet and made him head over everything for the church. [23] The church is his body, the fullness of him who fills everything in every way.**

Jesus once said, "Blessed are the pure in heart, because they will see God" (Matthew 5:8). We see things not so much with our eyes but *through* our eyes and *with* our hearts. This explains why many little boys think their mothers are prettier than Miss America. They see their moms *through* their eyes and *with* their hearts.

"I pray that the eyes of your heart may be enlightened," says Paul. It's as though we are sitting in a very dark room, surrounded by all kinds of wonderful things—but we don't see them. We don't know they are there. We can't enjoy them—until the Holy Spirit flips on the light.

When God enlightens the eyes of our hearts, when he brings us to believe in Jesus, we see things to which others are blind.

We see "the hope to which [God] has called [us]," says Paul—the sure and certain hope that when we lay our heads down on our pillows for the last time, the angels will carry our souls home and on the Last Day the voice of Jesus will call once more and reunite our risen bodies with our souls forever in heaven.

When God enlightens the eyes of our hearts, we see what spiritual billionaires we are in Christ. We see "how rich his glorious inheritance among the saints is": what rich kids we are in this world as the baptized and forgiven sons and daughters of the King and what an inheritance in glory we have waiting for us.

When God enlightens the eyes of our hearts, we see what kind of power it took to make Christians out of us—the same power it took, says Paul, to call Christ out of his grave on Easter morning—this Christ who now sits far above all earthly power with all things under his feet. Anybody who messes with his people, with his church, must now deal with him.

How different the eyes of faith are from the eyes of unbelief! Faith sees God's strength in a thunderstorm. Unbelief sees only broken branches. Faith sees God's love in a newborn baby. Unbelief sees only another mouth to feed. Faith sees God's purposes even in pain. Unbelief sees only reasons to blame God. Faith sees life as a journey home to God. Unbelief sees a person's few short years as the good, the bad, and the pointless. Faith sees the handwriting of God on the pages of Scripture. Unbelief sees one more pious myth. Faith sees sins washed away in the gospel waters of Baptism. Unbelief sees mere religious ritual. Faith sees the body and blood of Christ in bits of bread and sips of wine. Unbelief sees nothing. Faith sees God in a crib at Bethlehem and on a cross at Calvary. Unbelief sees an unfortunate prophet of some sort who ran afoul of the authorities. Faith sees what others cannot see—a Savior virgin-born, crucified, dead, buried, risen, ascended; the forgiveness of sins; an invisible kingdom of believing hearts; the presence of God in the darkest valleys; and the angels of God standing guard around our beds.

A pastor's prayer—thanking God for the faith already given, asking that we may know God even better, and praying that the Holy Spirit may pour down more and more light so we may see even more clearly how good we've got it as the royal family of the King. This prayer will not go unanswered—even among us.

2:1-10
Dead or Alive

In the Old Testament, the prophet Ezekiel pictures the people of Judah, to whom the Savior had been promised, trudging to Babylon in chains as a long line of POWs. They doubtless think: "Stick a fork in us. We're done. Our nation is as good as dead. Our hope of a coming salvation is dead too." They say: "Our bones are dried up. Our hope is lost. We have been completely cut off" (Ezekiel 37:11).

But the God who brings life out of death gives a vision of hope to Ezekiel. He shows Ezekiel a valley covered with bones, very dry bones—the bleached and scattered bones of people long dead. The Lord asks the prophet, "Son of man, can these dry bones live?" (Ezekiel 37:3), as in, "So, what do you think? Are these guys going to get up and walk around anymore?"

Fearful of underestimating the God of impossible cases, the humble prophet replies, "Lord God, you know" (Ezekiel 37:3). Then, at God's command, Ezekiel prophesies—speaks the Word of God—over the white and scattered bones. Suddenly, there is a rumbling, shaking, and rattling. Scattered bones come flying back together until the floor of the valley is filled with fully assembled skeletons. Then, as the prophet watches, tendons and flesh begin to blanket the skeletons. Now the valley is covered with countless cadavers—lifeless bodies. Then, just as when God breathed into Adam the breath of life—the breath of God, the wind of God—the Spirit of God enters these bodies. They spring to their feet. Fully alive! A mighty army!

That's the vision. Our first guess may be to relate Ezekiel's vision to the resurrection of all flesh on the Last Day. But the Lord himself says this is something that happens before the Last Day. He says, "These bones are the whole house of Israel" (Ezekiel 37:11). Then he makes a promise to the people of Israel: "I will put my Spirit in you, and you will live" (Ezekiel 37:14).

No matter how dead and done they think they are as the chosen people of God, God can still breathe life into them. God can still bring them back from their captivity in Babylon. God can still settle them in the land of promise again. God can still raise them up from the grave of their hopelessness. And God did. After 70 years of captivity, God brought them home again.

Here in the second chapter of Paul's letter to the Ephesians, Paul says that what God did for his ancient people in bringing them back to life again as a nation and in bringing them up from the grave of their captivity, he has also done for you and me in a far greater way. It is a matter of being dead or alive.

Listen to what Paul says:

¹You were dead in your trespasses and sins, ²in which you formerly walked when you followed the ways of this present world. You were following the ruler of the domain of the air, the spirit now at work in the people who disobey. ³Formerly, we all lived among them in the passions of our sinful flesh, as we carried out the

2:1-10 Dead or Alive

desires of the sinful flesh and its thoughts. Like all the others, we were by nature objects of God's wrath.

"You were *dead* in your trespasses and sins," says Paul. When the Bible uses the word *dead* to describe you and me as we are by birth and nature, without Christ, this is not just an exaggerated figure of speech, what your English teacher would call a hyperbole. God means it. We were conceived and born "dead in . . . trespasses and sins."

It goes back to what God told Adam and Eve: "You shall not eat from the Tree of the Knowledge of Good and Evil, for on the day that you eat from it, you will certainly die" (Genesis 2:17). We may say, "Yes, but Adam and Eve didn't die the moment they disobeyed God." Yes, they did. No, they didn't drop over dead physically. But we tend to think wrongly about death. The Bible does not speak of death as a state of nonexistence or annihilation. The Bible speaks of death as a real existence marked by separation. *Physical death* is the separation of body and soul until the day of judgment. Ecclesiastes says, "The dust goes back into the ground—just as it was before, and the spirit goes back to God who gave it" (12:7). *Spiritual death* is a separation from our friendship, our life, our relationship with the One who made us and bought us. Call it original sin, enmity against God, or being under God's judgment. It's what Paul means when he says we were "dead in . . . trespasses and sins." *Eternal death* is a conscious existence of everlasting, unending separation from the blessings of God. The book of Revelation sometimes calls this "the second death" (20:14). It's another name for hell. This too is not a state of nonexistence. That's the terrifying nature of it. It is a real existence, but forever apart from a life with God.

When a wife sees her husband snoring on the couch, she might remark that he is "dead to the world." He still exists, but he is oblivious to, unaware of, and uncaring of anything going on around him. That's the way it is with people who are dead to God. Paul says they live according to the ways of this world, according to the prevailing attitude of the world, insensitive to the Word of God and the love of God—dead to God. Some people might refer to this as "the spirit of the times" or "the in thing." They excuse their goatish, godless attitudes and actions with the tired old line "Everyone is doing it." Paul explains his reference to Satan as "the ruler of the domain of the air" and "the spirit now at work in the people who disobey," literally, "in the sons of disobedience." In other words, by nature we are the sons and daughters of our self-chosen father, the devil—chips off the old block. Satan's influence permeates human hearts as the air permeates the world around us.

It isn't just the other person somewhere out there who is "dead." Paul is talking about all people as they are by birth and nature, apart from faith in Christ. He includes himself when he says, "Formerly, we all lived among them in the passions of our sinful flesh, as we carried out the desires of the sinful flesh and its thoughts. Like all the others, we were by nature objects of God's wrath."

Here is the Bible's blunt diagnosis of what ails the human race. It is this massive and unapologetic assertion of original or inherited sin that by nature, as we are without faith in Christ, we are enemies of God and dead to God. We may not like to hear this. We may prefer the sweet soft drink the world feeds us—that we are basically noble, inherently good, and that whatever evil there is can be blamed on society (society, by the way, is made up of people) or a glitch in our glands. But the Bible's analysis is still the correct one. We see the marks of this vandalism on our nature in our wicked ways, our family fights, our foul mouths, and our stubborn hearts. We see the evidence in war, school shootings, grinding poverty, and false doctrines—the tokens of

2:1-10 Dead or Alive

people who are spiritually stillborn, walking corpses, strutting stiffs, and glamorous cadavers.

People without Christ may appear very active, alive, and involved. It's like the boy who watched his dad lop off the head of a chicken and, watching it running around, said, "Look, Daddy, he's dead and doesn't know it." Old movie fans may think of *Night of the Living Dead*—spiritual zombies. A younger generation may relate to the kid named Cole in *The Sixth Sense*. The boy says to Malcolm, the psychiatrist: "I see dead people." Malcolm says, "In your dreams?" Cole shakes his head. Malcolm says again, "Dead people, like in graves and coffins?" Cole shakes his head no again and then says, "Walking around like regular people. They don't see each other. They only see what they want to see. They don't know they're dead." Malcolm asks, "How often do you see them?" The boy replies, "All the time. They're everywhere." The world is full of dead people, a world of bleached bones. They're everywhere. They don't know they're dead.

But among the unsearchable riches of Christ is that you and I are no longer dead. We are alive! The Holy Spirit has brought us to life again through the gospel as it comes to us in the cleansing waters of Baptism, in the preached Word, and in the pardoning body and blood of Christ.

Here is how Paul puts it:

⁴But God, because he is rich in mercy, because of the great love with which he loved us, ⁵made us alive with Christ even when we were dead in trespasses. It is by grace you have been saved! ⁶He also raised us up with Christ and seated us with him in the heavenly places in Christ Jesus. ⁷He did this so that, in the coming ages, he might demonstrate the surpassing riches of his grace in kindness toward us in Christ Jesus.

Paul paints a bleak, black picture of the way we are by nature. Yet two words flood the picture with light: "But . . . God . . ." "But God, because he is rich in mercy, because of the great love with which he loved us, made us alive with Christ." Jesus talks about this in John 5:25-29. There, Jesus speaks of two kinds of resurrection—one is a resurrection from unbelief to faith, and the other is the resurrection of the body on the Last Day. In regard to the spiritual resurrection of coming to faith, Jesus says, "A time is coming and *is here now* when the dead will hear the voice of the Son of God, and those who listen will live" (emphasis added). In the gospel, you and I truly hear the voice of the Son of God, and we are no longer dead. We are alive.

"It is by grace [God's undeserved love] you have been saved!" says Paul. "Saved" as the Israelites were saved when they were trapped between the charging chariots of Pharaoh and the wild waves of the Red Sea with no way out, *but God* parted the sea and saved them (Exodus 14). "[God] also raised us up with Christ [his resurrection means a new life for us now and an unending life with him hereafter] and seated us with him in the heavenly places [*seated* us with him, as though it had already happened . . . so sure and certain is his promise of this resurrection on the Last Day!]" So throughout countless ages, God has continued to show each new generation the unsearchable riches of his grace. Dead or alive? There is no doubt which one we now are!

Here in these verses, which we have learned since childhood, is how Paul sums it up:

⁸Indeed, it is by grace you have been saved, through faith—and this is not from yourselves, it is the gift of God— ⁹not by works, so that no one can boast. ¹⁰For we are God's workmanship, created in Christ Jesus for good works, which God prepared in advance so that we would walk in them.

2:1-10 Dead or Alive

We may assume we know what the word *grace* means, and we assume also that others mean the same thing as we do when they use the word. Grace, as the Bible uses the word, is not an ability that God pours or infuses into us, thus enabling us to somehow score points with God. Grace is God's undeserved love—a pure gift. Grace is not just getting something for nothing. Grace is getting the very opposite of what we had coming. This is what makes grace so amazing.

Here again, it is good to remember, as we noted already in regard to the word *grace* in 1:2, that the Scriptures clothe the word *grace* with flesh and bones. Lest we allow the word to become a thoughtless cliché or shopworn jargon, let us recall that grace is King David bowing his broken and penitent heart beneath God's undeserved pardon after his shameful and sordid affair. Grace is the woman at Jacob's well finding that Jesus could freely quench the thirst in her soul that five husbands and a live-in lover could not satisfy. Grace is Zacchaeus leaving behind his doctored account books for the pearl of great price. Grace is a criminal crucified next to Jesus with no time left to make up for anything, with only a plea of repentant faith: "Jesus, remember me." Grace is the prodigal son trudging home, all his options played out, smelling of the pigsty where he had landed, falling into the open arms of his father. Grace is the great persecutor of God's people becoming the great apostle to the Gentiles. Grace is the undeserved gift of salvation and service given to every believer. Grace is not just getting something for nothing. It is getting the very opposite of what we have coming. Grace is "chief of sinners though I be, Jesus shed his blood for me" (CW 578).

We are saved by grace *through faith*. This salvation, won once for all people by the life, death, and resurrection of Christ, becomes ours personally through a simple, God-given, childlike faith in Jesus Christ. In fact, says Paul, this entire salvation—even the faith that believes this grace—is not from ourselves.

It too is the gift of God—not by works, not by any decision that we made, for corpses don't make decisions any more than Lazarus could raise himself from the dead (John 11). The Holy Spirit alone brought us to faith through the gospel, the means of grace. As Jesus put it, "You did not choose me, but I chose you" (John 15:16). Or as Paul put it, "No one can say, 'Jesus is Lord,' except by the Holy Spirit" (1 Corinthians 12:3).

So where do good works fit into the life of a Christian? Just as God created the sun to shine and apple trees to have apples, so he created Christians through the gospel to do good works. The term *created* emphasizes something only God can do. We are God's workmanship, God's work of art, created in Christ Jesus for good works. We are saved by grace, through faith, *for* or *unto* good works. Think about this: Who gets the credit for a beautiful painting? The canvas? The brush? The paint? No. The artist gets the credit. We even refer to a painting by the name of its artist—a Rembrandt, a Picasso, a Michelangelo. Who gets the credit for a poem, a novel, a play? The pen? The ink? The paper? No. The writer—Shakespeare, Dickens, Hemingway. Christians are God's masterpieces, re-created by God himself through the means of grace. As Luther allegedly put it, "You don't have to lecture your pear tree to have pears." It is a pear tree. It will have pears. Water is wet. Grass is green. Christians do good works—not in order to be saved but because Christ has already saved them.

These good works, says Paul, are what "God prepared in advance so that we would walk in them." From sharing the gospel to honoring your parents, from reading the Bible to cleaning the garage, from keeping yourself pure to doing your homework, from helping the helpless to cheerfully enduring adversity, from loving your spouse to organizing the house—God prepared all these things *in advance* for us to do. Wherever we find ourselves each morning, whatever challenges we face each day, big or little, all these things are God's assignments for us, God's opportunities for us, God's telegrams to you and me informing us that we are here for a reason. We are no longer dead, but we are alive for a purpose. Isn't it great to be alive!

EPHESIANS

2:11-22
All in the Family

You have been planning a family reunion for a couple of years. You reserved a shelter at the park. Now you put the picnic tables together and set out the beans and potato salad. The burgers and brats are coming off the grill. You're enjoying a cold one from the cooler as you stretch out in a lawn chair. You're laughing and telling tall tales about the old days.

But then you look toward the tables and are a bit stunned. You see an unkempt, unshaven fellow—obviously a transient. Did he just hop off a train? Does he have a rap sheet? When's the last time he had a bath? Who knows what kind of diseases he might carry?

The man steps up to the table, grabs a plate and a fork, and starts going through the line. He loads up his plate like someone who has not eaten in a long time. He plops himself down on your brother's lawn chair and starts eating. As the TV series with John Quiñones puts it, "What would *you* do?"

Perhaps you wonder about what you *should* do as opposed to what you *would* do. Chances are, one of the more take-charge relatives would promptly tell the man that it is a private family gathering, that he is welcome to take a few sandwiches and a cup of coffee, but then he should be on his way. Perhaps a few mothers might make comments about the safety of the children.

We may not think much about it, but this disheveled, whiskery hobo has feelings too, even if he is quite used to this reaction. No matter how he may have gotten himself into his vagabond life, he doubtless feels dejected and rejected, unwelcome and unloved. At the very least, he probably envies you—not only your creature comforts but also the blessing of belonging to a family.

This is very much the way things once were between God's chosen people of Israel and all those outside that special family, aka the non-Jews, the Gentiles. In the early church, as the gospel of the crucified and risen Savior brought both Jews and Gentiles to faith, those of Jewish blood looked with fear and suspicion at the Gentiles who were invited to sit down at the feast of salvation with the family of Abraham, Isaac, and Jacob. It may be that the Gentiles felt like wallflowers and fifth wheels at the family reunion.

A good many of the Ephesian believers to whom Paul writes this letter are new to the table, new to the family. They are gentile believers in Christ who now sing hymns and say prayers alongside Jewish believers, who now believe that Jesus is their long-awaited Messiah. By the blood of Christ, the old walls, the old barriers that once divided Jews and Gentiles, have come crashing down. To borrow the name of an old TV series in which redneck Archie Bunker and his hippie son-in-law live under the same roof, these Jews and Gentiles, you and I too, are now "all in the family."

Paul tells us that there is an inseparable link between how God made us members of his family and family members to one another in the holy Christian church:

2:11-22 All in the Family

> ¹¹Therefore, remember that at one time, you Gentiles in the flesh—the ones who are called "uncircumcised" by those called "the circumcised" (which is performed physically by human hands)— ¹²remember that at that time you were separated from Christ, excluded from the citizenship of Israel, and foreigners to the covenants of the promise. You were without hope and without God in the world. ¹³But now in Christ Jesus, you who once were far away have been brought near by the blood of Christ.

Until Christ actually came and completed the work of our redemption, there was a very real wall or fence in place between Jew and Gentile.

God himself had placed that barrier there. He told the people of Israel: "The LORD your God has chosen you to belong to him as a people that is his treasured possession, chosen from all the peoples that are on the face of the earth" (Deuteronomy 7:6). God himself had built a fence, a hedge, a wall of rules and regulations, of ceremonies and sacrificial observances, around Israel—so much so that Israel was truly an oddball among the nations, a fifth wheel in the ancient worldview. God wanted it that way to prepare his people for a coming Savior, to preserve alive the promise of the coming Messiah.

Yet God had also told his people that it would not always be that way: "Nations will walk to your light, and kings to the brightness of your dawn" (Isaiah 60:3). Or, as Paul draws on another verse from Isaiah (57:19), those once far away would be brought near by the blood of Christ.

Certainly, it is not only in our New Testament age that we meet believing Gentiles who look in faith to the promised Savior. Melchizedek came out of nowhere in the days of Abraham and was priest of God Most High, says the Bible. The Queen of Sheba

EPHESIANS The Unsearchable Riches of Christ

returned home to her people with reports of Solomon's wisdom and Solomon's Savior. Na'aman the Syrian went home to tell what great things God had done for him through the prophet Elisha. Jonah, the reluctant missionary, saw the entire city of Nineveh bow low in repentance. The 70-year captivity of the people of Judah actually helped spread the teachings of the one true God throughout the ancient world. Wherever the Jews were dispersed, a synagogue sprang up—and in every synagogue, a copy of the Scriptures. It is not so surprising that the wise men came from the east looking for the newborn King of the Jews. Nor should the faith of the Roman centurion in the gospels or of a gentile soldier named Cornelius in the book of Acts come as a surprise to us.

But for all that, Gentile believers were still barred from full participation. They were, in a sense, second-class citizens—

looking in from the outside—until the fullness of time would finally come. The Gentiles in general, the so-called "uncircumcised"—those not bearing the brand of Abraham—were without hope and without God in the world. The wall between the Gentiles and the Jewish nation was evident even in the literal wall in the temple of Jesus' day. Gentiles could not pass beyond the court of the Gentiles

upon penalty of death. The self-righteous bent of many Jews did not help matters any. You can only imagine how left out, how alienated from God's people, a man like Cornelius must have felt.

Those of us not physically descended from Abraham cannot appreciate this enough: Christ has given us also the right to call God our Father. He has broken down the barrier of our sin and broken down the wall of separation between Jewish and gentile believers, counting us all in the family.

2:11-22 All in the Family

Here is how Jesus did it:

¹⁴For he himself is our peace. He made the two groups one by destroying the wall of hostility that divided them ¹⁵when he abolished the law of commandments and regulations in his flesh. He did this to create in himself one new person out of the two, in this way making peace. ¹⁶And he did this to reconcile both to God in one body through the cross by putting the hostility to death on it. ¹⁷He also came and preached peace to you who were far away and peace to those who were near. ¹⁸For through him we both have access to the Father by one Spirit.

In hauntingly beautiful words, Christ once said, "And I, when I am lifted up from the earth, will draw all people to myself" (John 12:32). By his own body on the cross, Jesus put to death the centuries-long hostility between God and humans and between Jew and Gentile.

In a clear statement of the doctrine of the Trinity, Paul says that through Christ, the Son, both Jews and Gentiles have access to God the Father by one Spirit. This access was spelled out when Christ died and the veil in the temple was torn in two from top to bottom. The way to God is now open. That way is the same for both Jew and Gentile—through faith in Jesus Christ, humanity's substitute, who kept the commandments we have failed to keep, who died the death that should have been ours, who suffered the Father's wrath against sin so we may feel our Father's embrace, who walked out of the cemetery and pledged that we shall do the same.

The blessed result is that you and I, by faith in Jesus Christ, are now all in the family.

> **[19]So then, you are no longer foreigners and strangers, but you are fellow citizens with the saints and members of God's household. [20]You have been built on the foundation of the apostles and prophets, with Christ Jesus himself as the Cornerstone. [21]In him the whole building is joined together and grows into a holy temple in the Lord. [22]In him you too are being built together into a dwelling place for God by the Spirit.**

Here too we see the unsearchable riches of Christ, his amazing grace. You and I are no longer outsiders looking in. No longer illegal aliens but fellow citizens with God's people, members of God's household. This household, this family, is what we are talking about every time we confess in the Apostles' Creed that we believe in "the holy Christian Church, the communion of saints."

The holy Christian church, or communion of saints, is really the one true church. It is made up of all believers in Christ—and only believers in Christ. We call this one holy Christian church by another name: the invisible church—invisible because only God knows who truly believes in Jesus as their Savior. This family, ultimately visible to God alone, is as real as the invisible air that we breathe. We rejoice to know that there are such believers all over the world in many different Christian churches and that all Christians will enjoy perfect fellowship in heaven.

But we cannot attend an invisible church. We live our lives in the visible church, painfully aware that false teachings have caused tragic divisions in the visible church from the very beginning and that church bodies once orthodox or right-teaching no longer are. The ecumenical answer to this tragedy is to agree to disagree, to pretend that doctrinal differences are no big deal, to gather everyone under one big umbrella for a phony sort of unity, and to share altar, pulpit, and prayer fellowship without first agreeing on what the Bible teaches.

2:11-22 All in the Family

However, it is infinitely more loving to recognize that the church is built "on the foundation of the apostles and prophets," that is, upon the Holy Scriptures of the Old and New Testaments, "with Christ Jesus himself as the Cornerstone." The church thrives and grows only to the extent that it remains faithful to the Bible. Real unity exists only when those who kneel at the same altar agree on the same teachings of the Bible.

You and I and all believers—Jews and Gentiles—are stones in this living temple. It is a living building with living stones, as Peter reminds us in his epistle (1 Peter 2:4). God adds another stone to this building every time a baby is baptized and every time a person repents and turns to Christ in faith. You and I, individually and together, are dwellings in which God lives by his Spirit through the gospel in Word and sacraments. And lest we living stones become loose and fall out of the building, the Spirit is continually engaged in spiritual tuck-pointing, sustaining and repairing us as we stay close to the gospel in Word and sacrament, in Bible reading, and in Christian education. God never wants us to be outsiders again.

Imagine being a child abandoned on the streets of 19th-century New York. Your immigrant parents died on the way to America. You have no money, no relatives. You can't speak English. You are a foreigner, an alien, unable to fend for yourself.

That's the way it was for thousands of orphans starting in 1850. They slept in alleys, huddling for warmth in boxes or metal drums. To survive, the boys mostly stole, ate rats, or rummaged through the garbage. The girls sometimes worked for prostitutes as panel thieves, ripping off the wallets of distracted customers. The problem was ongoing until Charles Loring Brace, a 26-year-old minister, organized the Orphan Train. He packed hundreds of orphans onto trains heading west, announcing to towns along the way that anyone could claim a new son or daughter as the Orphan Train passed through. By the time the last Orphan Train steamed west in 1929, about 250,000 children had found new homes and new lives. It's hard to say how well it worked out for each and every one of those orphans, but two such orphans became governors, a third became a congressman, and still another became a Supreme Court justice.

Something like this has happened in your life and mine . . . only infinitely less risky than a hit-or-miss orphan train. By the blood of Christ, you and I are no longer foreigners, aliens, outsiders, and orphans looking in on the family picnic from the outside. Now we are members of God's household. Now we are all in the family. And there's no place like home.

EPHESIANS

3:1-13
The Secret Is Out!

March 12, 1943. British Lieutenant General Frederick Morgan steps into a crowded elevator at Scotland Yard in London. He is on his way to his first meeting as the newly appointed chief of staff to the supreme Allied commander. The purpose of the meeting? To plan the invasion of Europe and bring World War II to an end. The project code name? Operation Overlord. *Initial* target date? May 1, 1944.

The plans were top secret, hidden from the hundreds and thousands of people who would eventually carry them out. The mass production of ships, planes, tanks, and ammunition stepped up. New and intensive training confronted the troops. Millions of tons of supplies were stockpiled in Britain. The British, Canadians, and Americans assembled almost three million men.

Most people knew something was up. They expected some sort of big move. But they did not know exactly how it would be carried out or when or where. All of this remained a mystery, top secret, until June 6, 1944, when the lid came off. The secret was no longer secret, and the mystery of the high command unraveled as almost 7,000 ships, including 4,000 landing craft, and about 11,000 aircraft converged over the English Channel, taking aim at Normandy on the coast of France. The secret was out! D-Day—the invasion of Europe to break the back of Hitler's Nazi Germany—had begun.

Again, everyone knew something was up. But no one could know the details until it happened. In similar fashion, here in Ephesians chapter 3, Paul says that "the mystery of Christ" was finally revealed by the Holy Spirit in the fullness time. It isn't that God's people did not know that deliverance was planned and on its way, that Christ was coming. But the precise how, when, and where was not as clear for Old Testament believers as it is for those of us who hold the complete New Testament. In God's good hour, his plan of salvation, long foretold in the Old Testament, finally unfolded: D-day—the day of God's deliverance! For all of us ever since, the secret is out. The secret is revealed *in Christ, for all people, through the church.*

The secret or mystery that the devil dreaded finally came to pass *in Christ:*

> **¹For this reason, I, Paul, the prisoner of Christ Jesus for the sake of you Gentiles— ²Surely you have heard of the administration of God's grace given to me for you, ³namely, that the mystery was made known to me by revelation (as I have already written briefly). ⁴When you read this, you will be able to understand my insight into the mystery of Christ. ⁵This mystery was not made known to people in past generations as it has now been revealed by the Spirit to his holy apostles and prophets.**

Here Paul begins to offer up a prayer for the Ephesian Christians. He says, "For this reason, I, Paul, the prisoner of Christ

3:1-13 The Secret Is Out!

Jesus for the sake of you Gentiles—" But then he breaks off mid-sentence to talk about something else. He doesn't pick up his prayer again until verse 14 when he starts all over again, saying, "For this reason I kneel before the Father . . . " and so on.

The Spirit-inspired and brilliant apostle knows all about proper grammar and sentence structure. Actually, there's a fancy word for this interrupting of oneself in mid-sentence to pursue another thought. It's called an anacoluthon. You and I do this all the time. When we are enthused about something, when our hearts are full and we are excited about several things, we may start with the main story but then interrupt ourselves to go down the rabbit hole of a side story.

What is it that so excites the apostle that he interrupts his own prayer to add a paragraph of explanation? It is this mystery, this secret revealed in Christ Jesus. Paul says, "Surely you have heard of the administration [the stewardship or plan] of God's grace given to me for you, namely, that the mystery was made known to me by revelation."

In novels and TV shows, so-called mysteries are most often solved by the brilliant reasoning of sleuths such as Sherlock Holmes, Jessica Fletcher, or Columbo. The Bible also speaks of "mysteries." The Greek word *mysterion*, from which we get the English word *mystery*, is used six times in Ephesians alone, including three times in the chapter before us, and repeatedly throughout the New Testament. Jesus speaks of "the mysteries of the kingdom of heaven" (Matthew 13:11). The apostles call themselves "stewards of God's mysteries" (1 Corinthians 4:1). Paul speaks of "God's wisdom that has been hidden in mystery" (1 Corinthians 2:7). Pointing ahead to the resurrection on the Last Day, Paul says, "Look, I tell you a mystery . . ." (1 Corinthians 15:51). In fact, the Bible uses the phrase "the mystery of this lawlessness" (2 Thessalonians 2:7) to describe the

Antichrist, and John describes the apostate church as "Mystery Babylon the Great" (Revelation 17:5).

In many places the Bible calls the gospel a mystery also—not in the sense that the cults and lodges of today use the word, as some secret rite shared only with a select few, but as a mystery or secret in the sense that it has to be revealed, uncovered, disclosed. The gospel is not something that can be discovered by research or brainy thinking. It cannot be uncovered by contemplating nature or by looking inside oneself. It cannot be found by the thinking mind, the seeing eye, the hearing ear. It is something that must be revealed by God himself. This God has done through his verbally inspired and inerrant Word on the pages of the Bible.

Paul says that the secret of our salvation, the mystery revealed in Christ, is something that "was not made known to people in past generations as it has now been revealed by the Spirit to his holy apostles and prophets." This mystery, or secret, revealed in Christ is simply the gospel, the good news of God's own Son, who put in a personal appearance on this planet to do over for us what we did wrong, to pay off for us on a cross what we could never pay, and to cheat death on Easter morning as a pledge that our own graves too will one day be empty.

So the secret is out. This secret, or mystery, is revealed *in Christ* not merely to a select few, not just to the Old Testament people of promise—the Jews—but to the Gentiles also, to you and me too. It is revealed *for all people*.

> **⁶This mystery is that in Christ Jesus the Gentiles are fellow heirs, members of the same body, and people who also share in the promise through the gospel. ⁷I became a servant of this gospel, in keeping with the gift of God's grace that was given to me by the working of his power. ⁸To me—even though I am the very least of all the saints—was given this grace: to preach to**

the Gentiles the unsearchable riches of Christ ⁹and to enlighten everyone about the administration of this mystery. In past ages this mystery remained hidden in God, who created all things.

Here is another facet of this secret according to Paul: "This mystery is that in Christ Jesus the Gentiles are fellow heirs, members of the same body, and people who also share in the promise through the gospel."

Take note of some key phrases about the Gentiles: "fellow heirs, members of the same body, and people who also share in the promise." It is true that the special code of laws given through Moses at Mount Sinai was given only to Israel and only until Christ came to fulfill all those ceremonies and sacrifices. As Luther bluntly put it, "God didn't call me out of Egypt." (The author noted this quote from a seminary professor.) That's a good thing to remember for those who want the United States to be a present-day Israel or who want today's Christians to follow Old Testament dietary and worship regulations, which were only intended for the people of Israel until Christ came. Those things are not for us.

But there are a lot of other things in the Old Testament—timeless truths that are repeated in the New Testament—not just for Israel but for all people of all time. Idolatry, murder, adultery, and theft will always be wrong. Worshiping only the true God, hearing his Word, honoring our parents . . . these things will always be right.

But what about the most beautiful words of all in the Old Testament, the gospel promises and the gospel comfort of the coming Savior? Are these sweet things, comforting things, pardoning things meant for you and me too?

What about Psalm 23: "The Lord is my shepherd; I shall not want. . . . Yea, though I walk through the valley of the shadow of death, I will fear no evil: for thou art with me" (KJV)? Are those words spoken to you and me or only to the people of David's day? Or what about the comforting words of Isaiah, that evangelist of the Old Testament?

- "Come now, and let us reason together, says the Lord. Though your sins are like scarlet, they will be as white as snow. Though they are as red as crimson, they will be like wool." (1:18)

- "Those who wait for the Lord will receive new strength. They will lift up their wings and soar like eagles. They will run and not become weary. They will walk and not become tired." (40:31)

- "Do not fear, for I am with you. Do not be overwhelmed, for I am your God. I will strengthen you. Yes, I will help you. I will uphold you with my righteous right hand." (41:10)

- "Now this is what the Lord says, the Lord who created you, O Jacob, the Lord who formed you, O Israel. Do not be afraid, because I have redeemed you. I have called you by name. You are mine. When you cross through the waters, I will be with you. When you cross the rivers, they will not sweep you away. When you walk through fire, you will not be burned, and the flame will not set you on fire. Because I am the Lord your God, the Holy One of Israel, your Savior." (43:1-3)

- "I, yes I, am he. I blot out your rebellious deeds for my own sake, and I will not remember your sins." (43:25)

- "Until your old age, I am he, and until you have gray hair, I myself will hold you up. I myself made you, and

3:1-13 The Secret Is Out!

I myself will lift you up. I myself will hold you up, and I will rescue you." (46:4)

- "Zion said, 'The Lord has abandoned me. The Lord has forgotten me.' Can a woman forget her nursing child and not show mercy to the son from her womb? Even if these women could forget, I will never forget you. Look, I have inscribed you on the palms of my hands. Your walls are never out of my sight." (49:14-16)

- "Even if the mountains are removed, and the hills are overthrown, my mercy will not be removed from you, and my covenant of peace will not be overthrown, says the Lord, who is showing you mercy." (54:10)

These are but a very tiny sampling of the kinds of comforting words given to God's people throughout the Old Testament. But are these words meant for you and me too? Did God mean us when he said through the prophet Micah, "Who is a God like you, who forgives guilt, and who passes over the rebellion of the survivors from his inheritance? He does not hold onto his anger forever. He delights in showing mercy. He will have compassion on us again. He will overcome our guilty deeds. You will throw all their sins into the depths of the sea" (7:18-19)?

In our weaker moments of doubt, perhaps this thought occurs to you: These sweet promises from God must have been set down only for the Israelites, right? They were a pretty exclusive club. God can't mean me. He knows what I am really like. And God didn't lead me out of Egypt. I am not Jewish. I am a Gentile. What makes me think that I have an admission ticket to this special club, that God was thinking of me at all when he said such beautiful things to one particular group of people thousands of years ago?

But the secret is out, says Paul: "This mystery is that in Christ Jesus the Gentiles are fellow heirs, members of the same body, and people who also share in the promise through the gospel." Here is our claim ticket to the promises given in all those Old Testament promises. Through faith in Christ, we are (as the Greek prepositional prefix "with" or "together" emphasizes three times in verse 6) heirs *together*, members *together*, sharers *together*. We receive the same inheritance, the same family ties, the same promises of pardon and paradise.

This secret, or mystery, of the gospel is for Jew and Gentile and, Paul says, it is also for him . . . a former persecutor of God's people turned apostle. Paul cannot find enough words to thank God for the gift of his grace. "To me—even though I am the very least of all the saints—was given this grace: to preach to the Gentiles the unsearchable riches of Christ."

Paul calls himself "the very least of all the saints." By inspiration of God the Holy Spirit, Paul wrote 13 books of the New Testament. Half of the book of Acts details his missionary journeys. One could argue that he was the greatest of the apostles and the greatest missionary who ever lived. In the end, he gladly gave up his life for the sake of Christ.

And yet he calls himself "the very least of all the saints," of all believers. Now, least is least, right? You can't get any less than "least." And yet Paul uses his own unique word here. Various English translations try to capture it with phrases such as "the very least" or "less than the least." English teachers might call it a comparative superlative, like saying, "You think you're the least? I am leaster than you are!"

It isn't false modesty. Paul painfully remembers, as he says to Timothy, that he was once "a blasphemer, a persecutor, and a violent man" (1 Timothy 1:13). It's been a long and wild ride since that day on the Damascus road when the risen Christ appeared in glory to Paul, calling him out of the night and into the light

3:1-13 The Secret Is Out!

and appointing him to preach the faith he had long labored to destroy. Paul knows who he is; he is a sinner of Christ's own redeeming—the "leastest" of them all.

Others who were summoned to Christ's service would nod their heads in agreement. They knew themselves better than others, their weaknesses and sins and doubts. They didn't step forward to begin the high calling of God. Moses argued with God that he was ill-equipped to confront Pharaoh and lead Israel out of bondage. Isaiah argued that he was a man of unclean lips. Jeremiah said he was too young. Peter fell at Jesus' feet, too embarrassed even to be in Jesus' presence: "Go away from me, because I am a sinful man, Lord," he said (Luke 5:8).

And then there was John the Baptist. Jesus himself paid high honor to the great forerunner, saying, "Among those born of women there is no prophet greater than John" (Luke 7:28). And again, "John was a lamp that was shining brightly" (John 5:35). But that is not how John the Baptist saw himself. Pointing to Jesus as the Lamb of God, the Christ, and the heavenly Bridegroom, John said this: "The one who has the bride is the bridegroom. But the friend of the bridegroom, who stands and listens for him, is overjoyed when he hears the bridegroom's voice. So this joy of mine is now complete. He must increase, but I must decrease" (John 3:29-30). John simply saw himself as the best man at the wedding, the friend of Christ the Bridegroom. The best man does not mope through the wedding service or cry in his beer at the reception because his best friend has found a bride. He does not expect that the bride will go home with him after the reception. John neither expected nor desired for himself the glory that belongs only to Christ. John was content to stand next to the Bridegroom, to introduce Christ to the world, and then to leave the stage—his duty done, his joy fulfilled. Christ alone was the theme of his life, as he said of Christ, "He must increase, but I must decrease."

So it was with Paul. It was never about him. It was about Christ Jesus and him crucified. So it is with every real ambassador of Christ. To servants of Christ who are "less than the least" is given the grace, the undeserved privilege, to proclaim the gospel.

These riches of the gospel-secret are "unsearchable," says Paul. Paul's word for *unsearchable* or *untraceable* has to do with footprints that you start to follow, and then you run across another set of footprints that crisscross, and then another, and another . . . until you can no longer trace them all. So it is with the riches of Christ's good news. We see the footprints of God's grace going off in so many directions that we cannot even keep track of all God's goodness to us in Christ. Before time was, before the Creator said, "Let there be," God knew your name and mine. He set the eyes of his love upon us and planned to give us a share of these riches before the first cry from our infant lungs. He knew everything there was to know about us—every sin that would haunt us, every chapter. He saw it all as he hung on the cross and said, "All this, for you . . . for you." He saw to it that someone brought us to find out about this, to believe this through his means of grace. He adopted us. He has kept company with us on the homeward march. On mountaintops of joy and in deep valleys of broken hearts, he has held our hands. When nothing else and no one else could help us, he has poured down on us the peace that passes understanding and the unbreakable promise of heaven. It is hard not to notice the fruit of this gospel in so many lives—in the crinkly eyes of the elderly couple who have stayed faithful to each other, in the happy and teasing toil of those who always show up to serve their Savior, in the simple but priceless habit of fathers and mothers, week after week bringing their

3:1-13 The Secret Is Out!

children to God's house. All this and heaven too. As the years evaporate, who of us can keep track of the unsearchable riches of Christ? God is so good!

The secret is out—the secret once hidden in the God who created all things (note the assumption that God created all things as taught in Genesis chapters 1–2). This secret is now revealed in Christ, revealed for all of us, Jews and Gentiles, and continually revealed *through the church* in the gospel in Word and sacraments until the end of time:

> **[10]He did this so that, through the church, the multifaceted wisdom of God might now be made known to the rulers and authorities in the heavenly places. [11]This was done according to the eternal purpose that he accomplished in Christ Jesus our Lord. [12]In him we can freely approach God with confidence through faith in him. [13]So I ask you not to lose heart because of what I am suffering for you, because it is your glory.**

In your life and mine, in the lives of our grandparents and great-grandparents—through countless generations—the multifaceted, many-sided wisdom of God in Christ has been made known through Christ's church. It has been made known where the Word, the water, and the blood have clued us in on the secret of how he loved us before time was. It has been made known by what he did to show that love on skull-hill outside Jerusalem and by that torn-open tomb in Joseph's lovely garden. The secret is out. Christ has landed on our shores, taken back our hearts, and set us free. Now, "in him we can freely approach God with confidence through faith in him." This secret lifts the burden, breaks the chain, mends the mind, and heals the heart. It is a secret we dare not keep.

EPHESIANS

3:14-21
Infinitely More!

In a touching scene on the pages of the Old Testament, the aging prophet Samuel preaches a farewell sermon to the people of Israel. He sets before God's people their checkered past. They had taken God's grace for granted over the centuries, grumbled against God's goodness in the wilderness, and behaved badly in the lawless days of the judges. Now they are demanding a king simply because, like some whiny children, they want to be "like all the other nations." The white-haired prophet pulls no punches. He tells it like it is. He tells them what it is going to be like if they fail to repent. But he does not leave them comfortless or hopeless. "Do not be afraid," he tells them. "You have indeed done all this evil. Nevertheless, do not turn away from following the LORD, but serve the LORD with all your heart" (1 Samuel 12:20). In other words, "God still loves you, still wants you, still holds out his open arms to you all day long." While setting aside his civil leadership of the nation, Samuel still promises to do what a prophet is called to do: "I will instruct you in the way that is good and right" (1 Samuel 12:23). Then, pointing them to God's empowering grace, he adds, "Considering the great things he has done for you" (1 Samuel 12:24).

The old man makes one other promise to them. He says, "As for me, it is unthinkable that I should sin against the Lord by ceasing to pray for you" (1 Samuel 12:23). That's a stunning statement when you think of it. The prophet says it would be a sin against the Lord not to pray for his wayward people. Samuel clearly saw such prayer as part of his prophetic calling.

We hear a similar sentiment as we warm our hearts over Paul's letter to the Christians at Ephesus. A larger part of Paul's ministry than we might think was a ministry of prayer. His letters are loaded with prayers for his congregations. Like Christ, who spent many a night in solitary places praying, Paul exerted a great deal of energy in laying hold of the promises of God for the spiritual strengthening of the flocks entrusted to him.

We have noted how Paul interrupted his own prayer to marvel at the mystery, the divine secret, of the gospel revealed in Christ for all people through all generations in the church. Now he picks up his prayer for the Ephesians where he left off. He folds his hands, bends his knees, and gives glory to the God who is able to do infinitely more than all we ask or imagine.

The things for which Paul prays are infinitely more than the things for which the Ephesians or you or I are inclined to ask:

[14]For this reason I kneel before the Father of our Lord Jesus Christ, [15]from whom the entire family in heaven and on earth receives its name. [16]I pray that, according to the riches of his glory, he would strengthen you with power through his Spirit in your inner self, [17a]so that Christ may dwell in your hearts through faith.

Humbly kneeling before the Father—of which any other fatherhood is only a faint echo—Paul prays that God, out of the

3:14-21 Infinitely More!

riches of his glory, out of the bottomless pockets of his grace, may strengthen the believers in their inner selves with power through his Spirit.

Our "inner self" is another name for the new man, or the new Christian nature that God created in us when he brought us to faith through the gospel. On the one hand, this new nature is created in the image of God and wants only what God wants. But this new nature also matures and grows stronger as it battles the old sinful nature that clings to our bones. Paul prays that "Christ may dwell in [our] hearts through faith." Neither the labors of our hands nor the reasoning of our brains can bring us near to God. It is the heart brought to life by the Spirit's CPR in the gospel that embraces Christ by faith, trusts in him alone, expects from him all good things, and, in fact, expects infinitely more than we are even inclined to ask from him.

It is this Spirit-given faith that comes to appreciate Christ's love more with each new morning. Paul says:

> **17bThen, being rooted and grounded in love, 18I pray that you would be able to comprehend, along with all the saints, how wide and long and high and deep his love is, 19and that you would be able to know the love of Christ that surpasses knowledge, so that you may be filled to all the fullness of God.**

You and I ask God for a lot of things. We ask him for daily bread and good health. We ask him to watch over our loved ones and to deliver us from a thousand things that scare us. The Father is listening. But our desires are often too weak. We ask too little. There are infinitely more important things for which we could ask.

Paul prays that our hearts may sink deep roots down into the love of God, that our faith may be built on the firm foundation of

God's love for us, and that we may be given the power to increasingly appreciate how wide and long and high and deep his love is for us.

Even the strongest Christians, sometimes especially the strongest Christians, are assaulted by Satan, who sows doubt in their hearts: "Does God really love me? Am I really a child of God? Perhaps Jesus died for all, but did he die for me? Jesus forgives sins, but what about that one sin that still rises to the surface of my memory every so often?"

Why is it that we are too often sad, afraid, downhearted, guilty, joyless, or angry? Isn't it because we have not fully laid hold of God's love for us by faith? Isn't it because the old nature within us prods us to wonder whether God is out to get us, whether God will take away with one hand what he gives to us with the other, whether some discouraging disappointment or a downturn in our health is a punishment from him? Satan wants us to doubt that God loves us. He wants us to interpret every bump in the road as God taking another poke at us for the sins of yesterday. He wants us to doubt whether Jesus was serious when he said, "It is finished."

That is why we can never hear it too often: God is love. Christ proved it. He signed it in blood. He sealed it with the empty tomb. He could not be more serious when he says to you: "I have loved you with an everlasting love. I have drawn you with mercy" (Jeremiah 31:3).

This is the "infinitely more" for which we fail to ask our Father. Or as Jesus put it, "How much more will your heavenly Father give the Holy Spirit to those who ask him?" (Luke 11:13). Paul's prayer is that we may come to know this love that surpasses human knowledge, that our fullness and completeness may be found in God himself.

This is not going to happen, of course, apart from regular hearing and study of the Word. The motto of the Reformation has always been *by grace alone, by faith alone, by Scripture alone*. But ignorance of the Bible among many who claim that heritage is an unfortunate fact. We see Christians of less-orthodox denominations knowing their way around the Bible with chapter and verse, while many who lay claim to the Lutheran Reformation haven't picked up a Bible or catechism since they took off their confirmation robes. This is not a compliment. It is a solemn admonition to make "Scripture alone" more than a slogan, to make Bible reading and worship attendance and the Christian training of our children a living and breathing part of our lives so that the prayer of the apostle may be answered for us too.

This is how God wants to give us infinitely more than we are inclined to ask from him. This is how we come to know how much we are loved, how to rightly apply the law and gospel to the individual circumstances of our lives, and how to rightly evaluate all the confusing stuff that gets thrown at us and our children from the godless world. This is how we are strengthened with God's own might to endure adversity, to be patient under afflictions, and to be joyful each day in the warm embrace of our Father. God wants us to have all this. He is able, and he wants to give you and me infinitely more than we have thought to request.

He is also able "to do infinitely more than we can ask or imagine," says Paul:

[20]Now to him, who is able, according to the power that is at work within us, to do infinitely more than we can ask or imagine, [21]to him be the glory in the church and in Christ Jesus throughout all generations, forever and ever! Amen.

The roll call of faith is filled with examples in which God did infinitely more than his children expected or imagined.

Consider some examples: God allows Satan to strike Job over and over. Health, wealth, and children are all gone. Amid all the unanswerable whys, what Job ultimately learns by faith is that God is just even when he smites and God is good even when we cannot understand him. The clouds part, and Job tastes a double portion of God's love in ways he never imagined.

Or think of Abraham. God could only come off as a cruel adversary when he asked Abraham to give back his son Isaac.

God seemed to twist the knife: "Now take your son, your only son, whom you love, Isaac . . . offer him there as a burnt offering" (Genesis 22:2). Yet Abraham went up the mountain, saying, "The boy and I will go on over there. We will worship, and then *we* will come back to you" (Genesis 22:5). Scripture says that Abraham "reasoned that God also had the ability to raise [Isaac] from the dead" (Hebrews 11:19). When God stayed the hand that held the knife, Abraham got his son back in a way that was better than he ever could have imagined.

Or think of Jacob, already struggling with the guilt of his past and his fears of meeting up with his estranged brother, Esau, when the preincarnate Christ literally leaped upon him in a midnight wrestling match on the banks of the Jabbok River (Genesis 32). For the rest of his life, Jacob would walk with a limp as a reminder of that night when he would not let go of God until God blessed him. God did, in ways Jacob never could have imagined.

Or think of Joseph, sold into slavery in Egypt by his brothers, lingering for years in Pharaoh's dungeon. All of his life was one big no as he awaited, by faith, God's yes. But Joseph would later use his experiences as a sermon to his brothers: "You meant evil against me, but God meant it for good" (Genesis 50:20). The good was infinitely more than Joseph ever could have imagined on that day years earlier when, as a teenager, he was dragged away in chains.

Jesus himself knows all about this. He, the only begotten Son of the Father, received nothing but a divine no. God the Father gave his only Son the silent treatment and the cold shoulder on Calvary's cross. The Father appeared as an enemy to his Son for our sakes: "My God, my God, why have you forsaken me?" But three days later came the ultimate, everlasting yes!

It was everything God had already promised. But it was infinitely more than we could have imagined . . . much like the heaven Christ has waiting for us. As an elderly lady in a nursing home once remarked to her pastor, "When we get to heaven, we're going to wish we had been there a lot sooner."

EPHESIANS

4:1-16
Family Ties

A young man in an orange jumpsuit tries in vain to hide his face from the hungry lens of the TV camera as he is led away in shackles from the courtroom. His parents understandably refuse to talk to the relentless reporters. They barricade themselves in their home. The young man's friends distance themselves. Everyone feels the shame of the leg-irons and handcuffs.

Paul writes the God-breathed words of this letter to the Christians at Ephesus "as a prisoner in the Lord." He is under house arrest during his first imprisonment in Rome and is awaiting trial before Caesar. The New Testament evidence indicates that Paul was eventually released, that he may have gone as far as Spain on a fourth missionary journey. But he would then be arrested a second time—and that time the dungeon door would open down the path to execution at the end of a Roman sword.

Paul is not ashamed of the chain that shackles him to a guard in this rented house in Rome (Ephesians 6:20; Acts 28:20). He is not embarrassed by the ties that bind him. They are, in fact, his badge of honor. He is shackled not for crimes but for confessing Christ. At the start of chapter 3, he called himself "the prisoner of Christ Jesus for the sake of you Gentiles." Here at the start of chapter 4, he calls himself "a prisoner in the Lord."

In the chains that bind him, Paul sees pictures of other bonds, such as the "bond of peace," as he calls it. He sees a portrait of the family ties that hold together the household of God by spiritual *unity*, spiritual *gifts*, and spiritual *growth*.

> **¹As a prisoner in the Lord, therefore, I urge you to walk in a manner worthy of the calling with which you have been called. ²Live with all humility, gentleness, and patience, bearing with one another in love. ³Make every effort to maintain the unity of the Spirit in the bond of peace. ⁴There is one body and one Spirit, just as also you were called in the one hope of your calling. ⁵There is one Lord, one faith, one baptism, ⁶one God and Father of all, who is over all, and through all, and in us all.**

There is a unity among God's people that goes far beyond outward union or cosmetic camaraderie. It is a unity anchored in a common faith in Christ Jesus.

To nurture this unity, Paul urges believers "to walk in a manner worthy of the calling with which you have been called." The word Paul uses for "worthy" suggests an old-fashioned scale—with faith in one pan of the scale and a Christian life in the other. Our Christian life balances, matches, and corresponds to our faith. We are saved by faith in Christ alone, but real faith is never alone. It always produces a life that, despite its weakness, corresponds to faith.

Our Christian behavior is always a work in progress. Until we go home to God, there will always be a civil war within us, the sinful nature in a shoot-out with the new Christian nature. But the grace notes of encouragement are always there in these letters of Paul. As Christ once brought his apostles down from the glorious Mount of Transfiguration to the plain below, so Paul takes us from the heights of God's love in the first three chapters of this epistle—God's grace and eternal choosing, his breathing into us spiritual corpses the breath of faith—to the plain of our everyday lives as members of God's family.

The great apostle is saying: "You need to know how much God has loved you—all the way to the cross and back again from the grave. You need to know the soaring truths of your salvation—that you are saved by grace alone through faith in Christ alone. But you can know all the Bible passages in the world and still miss the point. Live up to what God has made you to be. Live up to your *noblesse oblige*, as the French would say, according to your station in life. You are the baptized sons and daughters of the King of kings. You are members of God's royal family. You are expensive souls, purchased at the frightful price of God's own blood. Now walk in a manner worthy of the calling with which you have been called."

You can guard your unity, your family ties, says Paul, as you "live with all humility, gentleness, and patience, bearing with one another in love." Our unity is cultivated not by the cult of self but by thinking about others more than ourselves, by being patient or long-suffering with our mutual frailties, and by putting up with one another's weaknesses.

In our human frailty, we step on one another's toes. The ties that bind can fast become, as the late humorist Erma Bombeck put it, "the ties that bind . . . and gag." It's the little stuff that starts something. Families know this. Someone doesn't cap the toothpaste. Someone never picks up the socks. The kid hollers, "I cleared the table last time!" So it goes in the family of believers too. Friction starts over the little things. Someone fails to greet you at the church door. You favor the church remodeling project; someone else strongly feels it is wasteful and extravagant. You feel others are getting more recognition than you for their efforts, even though you know that getting recognized must never be the point.

So how do we keep this unity of the Spirit in the bond of peace? This *esprit de corps* among God's people? This spirit of cooperation? Our real unity is not something we manufacture. It already exists. It is God's gift. It is, after all, the *Spirit's* unity that he created when he brought us to faith through the gospel in Word and sacrament. The same Word that brought us *to* faith holds us together *in* the faith.

In beautiful fashion, Paul weaves the doctrine of the triune God into this unity: "one Spirit . . . one Lord [Jesus] . . . one God and Father." And then, in reference to the biblical number for the fellowship between God and people, the number 7, he uses the word "one" seven times here: "one body . . . one Spirit . . . one hope . . . one Lord, one faith, one baptism, one God and Father."

There really is such a perfect unity and fellowship of kindred hearts, family ties that can never be broken. We confess it regularly in the Apostles' Creed: "I believe in . . . the holy Christian Church, the communion of saints." The holy Christian church, or communion of saints, is really the one true church. It is made up of all believers in Christ—and only believers in Christ. This is worth repeating: All those who believe in Jesus Christ alone as their only Savior from sin are members of this one holy Christian church, the communion or fellowship of saints—regardless of the race, nation, or church body to which they belong.

But we also call this one holy Christian church by another name: the invisible church. Invisible because its membership is known only to God. Only God knows who truly believes in Jesus as their Savior. We rejoice to know that there are other

4:1-16 Family Ties

sheep all over the world in many different Christian churches and that all Christians will enjoy perfect fellowship in heaven. We rejoice when we encounter others who confess Jesus as their Lord and Savior.

But the invisible church is a gathering of hearts that only God can see. You and I are not God. So you and I can deal only with the *visible* church. After all, if you invite someone to church next Sunday and the person says, "Sure, where is it?" it won't help much to say, "Well, it's invisible."

When you want to know where to find believers in Christ, you have to look for what the church fathers called "the marks of the church." Or, if you live in deer hunting country, you may refer to "the tracks of the church." What are the marks, or tracks, of the church? The gospel purely preached and the sacraments rightly administered. Where these things are happening, we have God's promise that believers are present as God wills (Isaiah 55:10-11)—even though hypocrites may be mingled in that visible gathering.

So here we are, living our lives in the visible church, painfully aware that there have been tragic divisions in the visible church from the very beginning and that church bodies once orthodox or right-teaching no longer are. The ecumenical answer to this tragedy is to agree to disagree, to pretend that doctrinal differences are no big deal, to gather everyone under one big umbrella for a shallow outward union instead of real unity—to share altar, pulpit, and prayer without first agreeing on what the Bible teaches. But such an approach is not as loving as it sounds. It is lacking in love for God and his Word, for the souls of others, and for our own souls.

Far more honest and far more loving is to first agree on the pure teachings of the Bible before kneeling at the same altar. This doctrine of God-pleasing church fellowship is the immune system of the visible church, warding off the lethal infection of false teachings, which the apostles compared to leaven (yeast) and gangrene (1 Corinthians 5:6; 2 Timothy 2:17). Such scriptural principles of church fellowship are not born out of the notion that some Christians are better than others, but just the opposite. It is because we are no better than others that we need to remember how susceptible we are to being misled. It is not without good reason that the entire Bible warns repeatedly against false teachings.

The family ties hold us together with spiritual gifts that promote this unity:

> **⁷But to each one of us grace was given, according to the measure of the gift from Christ. ⁸That is why it says, "When he ascended on high, he took captivity captive and gave gifts to his people." ⁹Now what does it mean when it says "he ascended," other than that he also had descended to the lower parts, namely, the earth? ¹⁰He who descended is the same one who ascended far above all the heavens, so that he might fill all things. ¹¹He himself gave the apostles, as well as the prophets, as well as the evangelists, as well as the pastors and teachers, ¹²for the purpose of training the saints for the work of serving, in order to build up the body of Christ. ¹³This is to continue until we all reach unity in the faith and knowledge of the Son of God, resulting in a mature man with a stature reaching to the measure of the fullness of Christ.**

The Savior who came down to earth to become one of us in all lowliness has now ascended far above all the heavens to fill all things. He has taken up the full use of his power to stand closer to us than our own shadows.

4:1-16 Family Ties

Here it might be mentioned that our Savior's ascension has often been misunderstood, as though when he ascended, he jettisoned his human nature like the second stage of an ascending rocket or, at least according to his human nature, is now confined to that place where angels and departed believers behold the vision of God.

When the Bible tells us that Christ "was taken up into heaven and sat down at the right hand of God" (Mark 16:19), it doesn't mean that Jesus is now confined to a fancy chair 3 miles left of Jupiter. The Bible uses the term "right hand of God" to describe the omnipresent exercise of all God's power. Our exalted Savior has now taken up the full and continual *use* of all the divine power that was given to his human nature at the very moment of his incarnation in the womb of the virgin Mary. Since his conception, Jesus Christ is and continues to be fully God and fully man in one person. By way of this personal union of the divine and human natures, Christ the man has always been in full *possession* of all divine power given to his human nature. In his state of humiliation, he chose, for our sakes, not to make *full and continual use* of this power. But in his exaltation, he has taken up the full use of this power.

What a comfort to know that Christ is present with us each day according to both his divine and human natures. Or as Luther once put it in his Christmas hymn: "Let hell and Satan rage and chafe; Christ is your Brother, ye are safe!" ("To Shepherds as They Watched").

Christ did not leave us empty-handed when he ascended to fill all things. As the psalmist foretold, Christ conquered his enemies, captured our hearts, and left behind others to continue his gospel presence through the ministry of the inspired apostles and prophets, through the ministry of evangelists—literally *gospelers*—who do mission work, and through the ministry of pastors and teachers of God's Word. All of these, in turn, train God's people "for the work of serving," for letting the light of the gospel shine wherever God has placed them—at the altars of their farms, offices, kitchens, and shops. This is done to "build up the body of Christ" until we all reach unity in the faith and in the knowledge of the Son of God and until we become more and more mature in faith. (Confer the biblical doctrine of vocation, which is how we serve God in our various callings in life, and the Table of Duties in Luther's Small Catechism.)

This is how these family ties hold us together by spiritual growth:

¹⁴The goal is that we would no longer be little children, tossed by the waves and blown around by every wind of teaching, when people use tricks and invent clever ways to lead us astray. ¹⁵Instead, speaking the truth in love, we would in all things grow up into Christ, who is the head. ¹⁶From him the whole body, being joined and held together by every supporting ligament, grows in accordance with Christ's activity when he measured out each individual part. He causes the growth of the body so that it builds itself up in love.

Those who have raised children know that infants have a short attention span. They will cry one moment . . . and laugh the next, forgetting why they were doing either. This is endearing in its own way. A mother delights in the cute way her child talks at age 2 or 3. But she would be quite concerned if the child spoke that way at age 14 or 24. There is nothing wrong with a six-year-old's knowledge of the Bible . . . for a six-year-old. So it is with

4:1-16 Family Ties

our spiritual growth. If our attention spans remain infantile, tossed back and forth by the waves, blown around by every wind of teaching, swallowing every crackpot idea that comes along with the latest book or deceptive TV preacher—until the next crackpot convinces us to change our beliefs—we stand to lose our very souls. The family ties are strengthened when we grow out of spiritual baby food to a greater love for the meat and potatoes of God's Word. Just as every child dreams of growing up, so it is the lifetime goal for you and me to grow up spiritually—with each part of the body growing and doing its own work to strengthen the family ties with spiritual *unity*, individual spiritual *gifts*, and spiritual *growth*. So, what do I want to be when I grow up? I want to be like Christ! God give us each a real growth spurt!

EPHESIANS

4:17-32
Get a Life!

You've heard people say it, haven't you? "Get a life!" You hear about old *Star Trek* fans—Trekkies—who spend much of their lives in the fantasy world of Captain Kirk and Mr. Spock. The story goes that the actor who played Kirk, William Shatner, somewhat with tongue in cheek, once told a convention of Trekkies: "Get a life!"

When you think of the way some people spend their few short years that God has given them on this earth, it's a shame, isn't it? Time is soon up. Then the door to eternity opens, and there are only two possible destinations. But you see people living for the weekend, for gaming, for the next drink, for money, for success, for sinful pleasures. Others live for that happy tomorrow when their ship will come in, but tomorrow never comes. They need to get a life.

In another letter to another group of Christians, Paul once said, "To live is Christ, and to die is gain" (Philippians 1:21). For Paul, to live was not to satisfy himself. To die was not to lose himself. Life was Christ. Death was gain. Only those who trust in Christ can say so. The only life worth living is the life lived by faith in Christ, in company with Christ, and for the sake of Christ.

Get a life! This is pretty much what Paul is saying to the Ephesian Christians. Being a Christian is not a matter of memorizing a few passages. It touches heart and life, all that we are and hope to be. If one truly believes in Jesus Christ, certain things imperfectly but inevitably follow when taking off the old life and putting on the new life—things as natural as apple trees having apples and water being wet. Paul is unafraid to set before each of us the inescapable conclusions of being a Christian:

> **[17]So I tell you this and testify to it in the Lord: Do not walk any longer as the Gentiles walk, in their futile way of thinking. [18]They are darkened in their understanding, alienated from the life of God, because of the ignorance that is in them, due to the hardness of their hearts. [19]Because they have no sense of shame, they have given themselves over to sensuality, with an ever-increasing desire to practice every kind of impurity.**

While some of the Christians in Ephesus were of Jewish background, many of them were of Gentile, that is, non-Jewish, background. They grew up in Greek and Roman cultures with no knowledge of the God of Israel and the Old Testament Scriptures that foretold a coming Savior. It is hard for any of us, humanly speaking, to shed the hidebound attitudes and the cultural baggage of the times in which we were raised. Paul emphatically tells the Ephesian Christians exactly what he tells us also: "So I tell you this and testify to it in the Lord: Do not walk any longer as the Gentiles walk."

In what respect? "In their futile way of thinking," that is, in the emptiness, the pointlessness, of their thinking. It isn't that a person without Christ cannot think. Some of the most brilliant and highly educated thinkers in the world are paraded in front of us on the TV screen or in university classrooms. But empty of Christ, their thinking is also empty, futile, and pointless—taking them only to the grave and an eternity without the blessings of God.

Without Christ, says Paul, people "are darkened in their understanding, alienated from the life of God, because of the ignorance that is in them, due to the hardness of their hearts." A few hundred years ago, Europe was all wrapped up in what became known as the Age of Enlightenment. The idea was that a human's brains, or reasoning powers, would, like some internal god, lead each person to the light. But that light within was darkness. That counterfeit lamp of inherently corrupt reason led humans to arrogantly deny the Creator and the Creator's Word.

Humans, by nature, do not pursue the true light. They run from it, as cockroaches scurry when someone flips on a light switch. It was Jesus himself who said, "The light has come into the world, yet people loved the darkness rather than the light, because their deeds were evil. In fact, everyone who practices wicked things hates the light and does not come toward the light, or else his deeds would be exposed" (John 3:19-20). There is a part of you and me that fears the candle of the Lord snooping around in the cellars of our hearts. Who of us wants to wear our whole life's story on our forehead for everyone to read? So we harbor the foolish hope that God himself cannot see in the dark, that we can go on walking in the darkness of unrepented sin and still sit at the Master's table. But in the dark, all things shrivel and die. I cannot see my Savior clearly if I deny the sin in my life, ignore it, rationalize it, excuse it, and flaunt it. Only in the light of him who loved me and poured out his life for me can I live and grow beneath the sun that cheers my spirit.

Read once more how Paul paints this old life without Christ:

[18]They are darkened in their understanding, alienated from the life of God, because of the ignorance that is in them, due to the hardness of their hearts. [19]Because they have no sense of shame, they have given themselves over to sensuality, with an ever-increasing desire to practice every kind of impurity.

Over the years, some have attributed the following quotation to Adolf Hitler: "I want to raise a generation of young people devoid of conscience—imperious, relentless, and cruel." Whether or not Hitler spoke those words, the expressed goal for that younger generation was what Paul means by such terms as "the hardness of their hearts" and having "no sense of shame"—literally, being past feeling or callous. Jeremiah said the people of Judah in his day had forgotten how to blush (Jeremiah 8:12). Like a leper whose limbs wear away because he feels no pain, life without Christ results in people giving "themselves over to sensuality, with an ever-increasing desire to practice every kind of impurity."

The Roman Empire of Paul's day didn't have a monopoly on this old way of life without Christ. All around us, we see the evidence of hearts that feel no pain—no pangs of conscience. For decades our own nation has heaped its defenseless unborn infants in dumpsters in the name of convenience. We have wiped our muddy feet on God's Sixth Commandment with recreational sex, often playing house in the line of sight of the children who are bound to follow suit in their own lives. We have given the name "marriage" to what the Scriptures call perversion.

4:17-32 Get a Life!

This is the world you grew up in, says Paul to the Ephesians. It is pretty much the world our children are growing up in too. But this is not how you learned Christ. Using the picture of taking off a rotten set of clothes and putting on a new suit, Paul says to the Ephesian Christians of old and to you and me too, "You can continually put off the old life, and you can continually put on the new life." Listen to Paul's words:

> **20But you did not learn Christ in that way, 21if indeed you have heard of him and were taught in him (since the truth is in Jesus). 22As far as your former way of life is concerned, you were taught to take off the old self, which is corrupted by its deceitful desires, 23and to be renewed continually in the spirit of your mind, 24and to put on the new self, which has been created to be like God in righteousness and true holiness.**

Think back, says Paul, to when you first got to know Jesus. What did you learn from him? Think back, my friends, to the Christ you first learned about in Sunday school or through the study of the Scriptures and the catechism in your younger years. Does the voice of Jesus seem strange to you now? Does the licensed living glorified on the glowing screen in your living room now seem normal and inviting? Would you invite such people into your home? That's the old life, not the new life you have learned from the One who bought you at the frightful price of his own blood.

It is time to "take off the old self, . . . to be renewed continually in the spirit of your mind, and to put on the new self, which has been created to be like God in righteousness and true holiness." God first made humans in his own image: wanting what God wants, thinking the thoughts of God after him, and agreeing with God. Humans derailed this relationship by trying to make God in their image. In Christ alone, this is reversed. In our daily walk with God, we want to be more and more like Christ: wanting what he wants, thinking what he thinks, loving what he loves, and hating what he hates. We daily drown the old Adam, the sinful nature, the old life, in the gospel waters of Baptism, remembering what God has made us to be: his children, chips off the old block.

Here are some examples, says the apostle, of how to take off the old life and put on the new life:

> **25Therefore, after you put away lying, let each of you speak truthfully with your neighbor, because we are all members of one body. 26"Be angry, yet do not sin." Do not let the sun go down while you are still angry. 27Do not give the Devil an opportunity. 28Let the one who has been stealing steal no longer. Instead, let him work hard doing what is good with his own hands, so that he has something to share with a person who is in need. 29Do not let any unwholesome talk come from your mouths. Say only what is beneficial when there is a need to build up others, so that it will be a blessing to those who hear. 30Do not grieve the Holy Spirit of God, with whom you were sealed for the day of redemption. 31Get rid of every kind of bitterness, rage, anger, quarreling, and slander, along with every kind of malice. 32Instead, be kind and compassionate to one another, forgiving one another, just as God in Christ has forgiven us.**

Always, while we live out our forgiven lives as the baptized sons and daughters of the King, there is this putting off the rags of the old life and this putting on the shining suit of the new life.

4:17-32 Get a Life!

There is to be no vacuum as we jettison the vices of the sinful nature. Nature abhors a vacuum.

So, put off falsehood? Yes. And then speak truthfully to our neighbors, for we are all members of the one body of Christ. Once we cannot count on one another to tell the truth—when spouses can't trust each other or parents can't count on their kids to tell them what really happened—our new life breaks down at the very foundation.

"Be angry, yet do not sin." There is a righteous anger of which the Bible speaks. Prophets, apostles, and Christ himself became righteously angry. But for you and me, who mud-wrestle with our sinful nature, sin is always on the threshold. Our sinful nature easily employs anger in its own arsenal to fuel ill will and hatred. So the apostle gives the advice that has kept a lot of marriages and friendships from running aground on the rocks: "Do not let the sun go down while you are still angry. Do not give the Devil an opportunity." So put off anger and put on peace.

"Let the one who has been stealing steal no longer"? Absolutely. But having stripped off that loveless vice, replace it with a better garment: honest labor. That way, you will have something not just for yourself but something to share with others in need, so they will not be tempted to steal either.

"Unwholesome talk"? Paul's "unwholesome" refers to the stench of rotting, dead fish. Yes, get rid of that language of the old life. James writes this in his little letter: "Blessing and cursing come out of the same mouth. My brothers, these things should not be this way" (3:10). We sing hymns and say prayers but then walk out the door of God's house to spew some pretty unbaptized vocabulary. Take that off. Replace your foul vocabulary with words that build up those around you with the law and gospel, with gentle guidance and encouragement.

And do not grieve the Holy Spirit of God with whom you were sealed, marked as his own for that day of ultimate redemption when he will shatter the last shackles that bind us and bring us to his new world. Put off all the bitterness, rage, anger, quarreling, slander, and malice that mark the old life, and put on the new life of kindness and compassion. Ponder the bottomless mortgage of sin that Christ canceled for us by his death on the cross, and forget the paltry pennies owed us by others for whom Christ also died.

Only by faith in him who became one of us—to be for us what we were not, to do for us what we could not, to die for us that we might not, to rise again from the grave that we might get a life—only by faith in him are we empowered each day to take off the old life and put on the new life. In that old life of bondage, it was said, "To run and work the law commands, yet gives me neither feet nor hands." However, in this new and free life of the Spirit, it is sung, "But better news the gospel brings; it bids me fly and gives me wings" (from a poem by an unknown author as quoted by Jason C. Meyer in *The End of the Law*, p. 2).

EPHESIANS

5:1-21
How Shall We Then Live?

In the ancient liturgical calendar of the Christian church year, the final Sundays are centuries-long reminders of our eventual rendezvous with our Redeemer—the final judgment and the final triumph of God's people through Christ our King.

For Christians, the Last Day colors every other day. For instance, the apostle Peter says, "Since all these things will be destroyed, what kind of people ought you to be, living in holiness and godliness, as you look forward to and hasten the coming of the day of God?" (2 Peter 3:11-12). In this letter to the Ephesian Christians, Paul says the same: "Consider carefully, then, how you walk, not as unwise people, but as wise people. Make the most of your time, because the days are evil" (5:15-16). We wake up each morning one day closer to forever. How shall we then live? Paul answers this in the light of *who we are* and *where we are going*.

Paul addresses the Ephesian Christians in terms of *who they are:* the baptized sons and daughters of the Most High.

> ¹Therefore, be imitators of God as his dearly loved children. ²And walk in love, just as Christ loved us and gave himself for us, as a fragrant offering and sacrifice to God.

"Be imitators of God as his dearly loved children." Paul uses the word from which we get the term *mimic*. In a thousand ways, for good or bad, to our delight or embarrassment, children mimic their parents. We talk about role models for children and young people. There is no better role model than God himself, who loved us enough to become one of us. There is no one better to mimic than Christ, whose entire life and death smelled sweet to God, who replaced our stunk-up lives with his fragrant life.

If the world is to notice any of our Savior's features in us, any of the family likeness in us, Paul needs to address some things that bear no resemblance at all to Christ:

> ³But do not let sexual immorality, any kind of impurity, or greed even be mentioned among you, as is proper for saints. ⁴Obscenity, foolish talk, and coarse joking are also out of place. Instead, give thanks. ⁵Certainly you are aware of this: No immoral, impure, or greedy person—such a person is an idolater—has an inheritance in the kingdom of Christ, who is God. ⁶Let no one deceive you with empty words. It is because of these things that the wrath of God is coming on the sons of disobedience. ⁷So do not share in what they do.

Paul makes no bones about the fact that some things are a contradiction of who we are. The life of love we are to live is not the same as the world's licensed lust. Paul says, "Do not let sexual immorality, any kind of impurity, or greed even be mentioned among you." Let the godless world point to us and say that we are narrow-minded Neanderthals, puritanical party poopers. So what! But let it never be said of us that we are as raunchy as the rest of the world. Such things should not even be mentioned among us. There should not even be a hint of such things among us. Sadly, there is often more than a hint of it among people who want to carry the name Christian. God's people ought not even allow the impression that they are toying with sex before or outside of marriage. After all, what kind of signal does that send? What sort of imitation of Christ is that?

Let there be no indication among us of the all-American lust for things, the idolatrous affair with the grinning god of materialism, the daily discontentment with what God has given us. This is not who we are as God's holy people. Obscenity, porn, smutty jokes, and gutter language—these do not fit who we are any more than King Saul's armor fit the shepherd boy David. These things are not neutral. They are evil.

"Certainly you are aware of this," says Paul. "No immoral, impure, or greedy person—such a person is an idolater—has an inheritance in the kingdom of Christ, who is God." Each of us struggles with our own festering brand of sin. We do battle daily with our own besetting weaknesses. The duel between the Christian nature within us and the sinful nature within us will not be over until we go home to God. But the Scriptures are clear. They are unequivocal. A soul that lives deliberately and defiantly in unrepented sin is not on the path to heaven but on the road to hell.

"Let no one deceive you with empty words," says Paul. "It is because of these things that the wrath of God is coming on the sons of disobedience. So do not share in what they do." Empty words are words without substance, without reality—words that try to dull the dagger of God's law. There is a relentless evangelism of evil that rewrites the dictionary. You can call lust love.

You can call fornication a meaningful relationship. You can call perversity diversity. You can call butchering unborn babies choice. You can call good evil and evil good. But these are empty

words. They are lies. You may even get all your friends and family members to agree with these lies. You may partner only with people who don't prick your conscience with the raw truth. You may even stay away from church like a kid holding his breath until he gets his way. You may go shopping for a new and improved church that is not so hung up on the plain words of the Bible. Either way, these empty words will be no

escape hatch when the wrath of God comes. Those who live like this have no inheritance in the kingdom of Christ, who is God.

But don't miss the grace note in that word *inheritance*. An inheritance is a gift earned for us by the life and labors of another. An inheritance becomes ours upon the death of another. An inheritance implies that you and I are the adopted sons and daughters of the King. It says that everything that belongs to him belongs to us. His perfect life is deeded to us. His payment for sin on the cross is transferred to our account. His resurrection is our passbook to life eternal. But we stand to lose this inheritance if we run away from the home of our Father to that far country where liberty *from* sin is morphed into a license *to* sin.

Clearly, says Paul, this licensed life of sin is not who we are.

⁸For you were once darkness, but now you are light in the Lord. Walk as children of light, ⁹for the fruit of the light consists in all goodness, righteousness, and truth. ¹⁰Try to learn what is pleasing to the Lord, ¹¹and do not participate in fruitless deeds of darkness. Instead, expose them. ¹²For it is shameful even to

> **mention the things that are done by people in secret. ¹³But everything exposed by the light becomes visible, for it is light that makes things visible. ¹⁴Therefore it is said, "Awake, sleeper, rise from the dead, and Christ will shine on you."**

It is pure gospel when Paul says to the Ephesian Christians, "You were once darkness, but now you are light in the Lord." Paul said something similar to the Christians at Corinth after giving them a laundry list of sinful behaviors. He told them, "Some of you *were* those types of people. But you were washed, you were sanctified, you were justified in the name of our Lord Jesus Christ and by the Spirit of our God" (1 Corinthians 6:11, emphasis added).

Do you hear a soothing sermon in the tense of the verb? "You *were* once darkness." Ironic, isn't it? The godless world is so generous in handing you a license *to* sin, but once you get tripped up by some sin—trapped in it—then the world is the first to hang a label on you for the rest of your life. It is the liberating Christ alone who tears off the label with one little word: *were*. "You *were* once darkness." But not anymore.

"Now you are light in the Lord." So how shall we then live? "Walk as children of light," says Paul. In the dark, we shrivel and die. In the light, we blossom and live. "I am the vine," says Christ, "ye are the branches: He that abideth in me, and I in him, the same bringeth forth much fruit: for without me ye can do nothing" (John 15:5 KJV). "The fruit of the light," says Paul, "consists in all goodness, righteousness, and truth." Search the Scriptures and find out what pleases the Lord. Because of who we are, what pleases the Lord pleases you and me. What pleases the Lord matters.

As far as the fruitless, lifeless deeds of darkness are concerned, shine the light of the Word on these creatures of the night and expose them for the shameful and vile things they are. Wake up, O sleeper, rise from the death of unbelief, and Christ will shine on you.

How shall we then live? Not only in the light of *who we are* as God's children but also in the light of *where we are going*.

> **¹⁵Consider carefully, then, how you walk, not as unwise people, but as wise people. ¹⁶Make the most of your time, because the days are evil. ¹⁷For this reason, do not be foolish, but understand what the will of the Lord is. ¹⁸And do not get drunk on wine, which causes you to lose control. Instead, be filled with the Spirit ¹⁹by speaking to one another with psalms, hymns, and spiritual songs (singing and making music with your hearts to the Lord), ²⁰by always giving thanks for everything to God the Father, in the name of our Lord Jesus Christ, ²¹and by submitting to one another in reverence for Christ.**

As in the parable of the wise and foolish virgins (Matthew 25), the cry resounds: "Look, the bridegroom! Come out to meet him!" When the Lord Christ returns, many will rise from their graves. Others will rise from their beds. Still others will get up from their benches and desks, from their bleachers and barstools, and, yes, from their pulpits and church pews. Some, having waited wisely by faith, will rise ready and joyful to meet the Bridegroom. Others, utterly beside themselves, will rise, filled with terror.

"Consider carefully, then, how you walk," says Paul, "not as unwise people, but as wise people. Make the most of your time, because the days are evil. . . . Do not get drunk on wine, which causes you to lose control." Some translations use the word *debauchery*, which is a word used elsewhere in the language of the New Testament. It is the word for the reckless living of that prodigal son in the far country (Luke 15:13). There's no need to explain. It's everywhere. How many homes and relationships have been torn to shreds by the abuse of alcohol or mind-altering substances?

Fill up on something else: "Be filled with the Spirit." The only pump where you get that fill-up is at the pump of the gospel in Word and sacrament—nothing more, nothing less, nothing else. You may think pastors harp a bit much on being present for regular worship, for Word and sacrament. But we all go through life filled with something. Nature abhors a vacuum. If it is not the Spirit of the living God through the gospel that fills us, it will be something else—something ugly, something that will not and cannot save us.

How shall we then live? Clearly, we want to live in the light of who we are and where we are going. To repeat, this is how Paul describes the ways in which being filled with the Spirit shows itself.

> **[19]... by speaking to one another with psalms, hymns, and spiritual songs (singing and making music with your hearts to the Lord), [20]by always giving thanks for everything to God the Father, in the name of our Lord Jesus Christ, [21]and by submitting to one another in reverence for Christ.**

Being "filled with the Spirit" bears fruit "by speaking to one another with psalms, hymns, and spiritual songs (singing and making music with your hearts to the Lord)," as we lift our grateful voices to the God of our salvation.

Being "filled with the Spirit" shows itself by "always giving thanks" for all the blessings of body and soul that our Lord pours out on us each day.

Finally, being "filled with the Spirit" unfurls itself "by submitting to one another in reverence for Christ." A word like *submit* grates like fingernails on a chalkboard in modern ears. The word Paul uses is an old military word that means "to line up under," sort of like "follow the leader." Throughout these verses, the King James Version rightly captures the so-called middle voice of the verb Paul uses, as in "submitting yourselves." So, this submitting is not a forced subjugation. It is a willing and voluntary submitting of one's self to another. It's what Christ did when he washed the feet of the disciples and then said, "You also ought to wash one another's feet" (John 13:14). I trust none of us would consider it demeaning to imitate Christ. It is an overarching principle in the household of God that we submerge our own interests for the sake of others and engage in service before self. This is what one Bible scholar called a "happy harmony" with "no rivalry, no self-exaltation, no divisive pride" (R. C. H. Lenski, *The Interpretation of St. Paul's Epistles to the Ephesians and Philippians*). This overarching attitude is born of the Holy Spirit in our Christian lives. In Ephesians 5:22–6:9, Paul shows how joyful submissiveness plays out in various areas of our Christian lives.

The voice of the Savior calls to his church, to you and me, on the pages of the Old Testament's Song of Songs: "'Arise, my darling, my beautiful one, and come.' Look! Winter is over. The rainy season has come to an end. Flowers appear in the land. The season of singing has arrived" (2:10-12). The long winter is over. What we *were* has melted away. What we *are* in Christ abides forever.

How shall we then live? By waiting for the sound of his voice: "Be of good cheer! It is I! Be not afraid! Arise and come with me!"

EPHESIANS

5:22-33

The Mystery of Christ's Love for Us Inspires Our Own

Walk up to a few people at a gathering and whisper, "Do you want to know a secret?" Every head will turn. Every ear will perk up. Of course they want to know a secret. And the only way they can know the secret is if you tell them.

This is how it is with the word *mystery* as the Bible uses it. In the Bible, a mystery or secret refers to something you cannot discover by thinking hard about it or searching long for it. The puzzle can be assembled, the mystery can be solved, and the secret can be revealed *only* by God himself. When Paul talks about how Christ saved us by a bloody and hideous cross, he calls it "God's wisdom that has been hidden in mystery" (1 Corinthians 2:7). It's a secret we never would have guessed if God had not revealed it on the pages of the Bible. When he talks about the resurrection on the Last Day, he says, "Look, I tell you a mystery" (1 Corinthians 15:51). If the Bible had not told us, we never would have imagined that God was going to raise us from our dusty graves and give us glorified bodies that will never grow old.

Here in his letter to the Christians in Ephesus, Paul employs the gospel mystery of Christ's love for his church and his people's joyful submission to his gentle leading as the ideal inspiration and example for the interaction of husband and wife. When Paul says, "This is a great mystery, but I am talking about Christ and the church," he is talking about the wondrous relationship between Christ and the church described by the Old Testament prophets who spoke of Israel as God's betrothed and conversely spoke of Israel's idolatry as spiritual adultery and unfaithfulness to God, the lover of their souls.

Paul has been writing to the Ephesians about the worldly neighborhood in which they live—dark and drunk, godless and greedy, lusty and lying. Their neighborhood is truly our own. But now he takes us by the hand, out of the noisy neighborhood, into the sanctuary of the Christian home. Here he shows us the mystery. The Bible says, "The guidance [KJV: "secret"] of the Lord is with those who fear him. His covenant will give them knowledge" (Psalm 25:14). In other words, we are going to appreciate this only if we first know Christ by faith. Only then will we say with a full heart, "Speak, Lord, for your servant is listening."

How such service before self plays out in a specific kind of submitting as we are "filled with the Spirit" (5:18) is here applied to Christian marriage:

> **22Wives, submit to your own husbands as to the Lord. 23For the husband is the head of the wife, just as Christ is the head of the church, his body, of which he himself is the Savior. 24Moreover, as the church submits to Christ, so also wives are to submit to their husbands in everything.**

Brides and bridesmaids have snickered, smirked, and slyly winked at one another as the preacher reads these inspired

5:22-33 The Mystery of Christ's Love for Us Inspires Our Own

words at the Lord's altar. Why is that? Partly because they have a distorted idea of what the Bible teaches about the roles of man and woman in general and about marriage in particular. They have allowed the godless world to define the Bible's view of marriage with a caricature, a cartoon image of this relationship—sort of a primitive Fred and Wilma Flintstone image. Their immediate reaction is one of ridicule or at least to be condescendingly amused that anyone would still take such Bible passages seriously.

Or maybe some are annoyed by such portions of God's Word because they fail to pay attention *to whom* God is speaking. This is a matter of submitting oneself, not a matter of forcing someone to submit. (Recall that throughout these verses, the King James Version rightly captures the so-called middle voice of the verb that Paul uses, as in "submitting yourselves.") Christian wives *want* to listen to what God is telling them to do. Christian husbands *want* to listen to what God is telling them to do. If a parent tells one child to sweep the floor and he objects that his sister was supposed to do the dishes, the most likely response of the parent is that the child better pay attention to what *he* was told to do. *God's* children need to guard against this very thing.

A fellow comes storming into the pastor's study and says, "Pastor, doesn't the Bible tell my wife to submit to me?" "Yes, Fred, but *to whom* is God talking? To your wife, not to you. What has God told *you* to do? To love your wife as Christ loved the church and died for her. Are you drawing your wife along with loving-kindness or driving her away with your constant put-downs and dictatorial demands?"

Or there is the wife who also has hearing trouble. "Pastor, isn't my husband supposed to love me more?" "No doubt about it, Agnes. But *to whom* is God talking? To your husband, not to you. What has God told *you* to do? To follow your husband's lead in everything in the way the church follows Christ. Are you making it easy for him to be the husband or pulling the rug out from under his leadership with constant criticism?"

If a husband is listening to what God tells him to do and a wife is listening to what God tells her to do, the competition and the silly caricatures melt away. All of this was a beautiful thing in the beginning. Adam and Eve were not trying to undermine each other's God-given roles. Only when sin entered the picture did man turn his loving headship into an ugly dictatorship and did woman turn her quiet spirit into "I am woman, hear me roar!" Only in Christ does all of this become beautiful again. Only from those who believe in Christ can we expect a joyful "Speak, Lord, for your servant is listening!"

Why do we find ourselves talking back to God himself about the "manufacturer's directions" for marriage? It is because the unbelieving world and, yes, our own sinful nature—the houseguest from hell within us—argue with God. This disagreement is often enhanced by certain pet sins or pet opinions that people hold to in a given time or place. If a missionary were to go to certain groups in Africa or other areas of the world and teach what the Bible says about the headship of the man and the submission of the wife, no one would bat an eye. The hard part might likely be to get the men to be more loving in their leadership. But no one in such societies would have a problem with God's order of creation. On the other hand, if that same preacher went on to explain to such groups that the Bible teaches "the *two* shall be one flesh," not "the three or four"—that one wife is enough for any man and that polygamy is contrary to God's original plan—he might get considerable pushback from his listeners.

Now, if a pastor were to teach the same Bible lesson to a group in an American or European setting, pointing out that God's ideal is monogamy, not polygamy, he would get few arguments. (Sadly, however, one has to convince many in our society that they should get married in the first place, that once married

5:22-33 The Mystery of Christ's Love for Us Inspires Our Own

they should stay married rather than engage in the progressive polygamy of promiscuous divorces, or that marriage should be a lifelong union between only a man and a woman.) But if a pastor preached on these words from Ephesians about the order of creation to his Midwestern congregation in the current politically correct atmosphere, he might encounter a fair amount of irritation and disagreement. After church, some of the members might add "roast preacher" to the menu. In one setting or another, the Bible is always countercultural.

You see, we bring our sinful natures, our pet opinions, and our cultural influences to the hearing of God's Word. This gets in the way of our seeing how God's will is good and right for us. But Paul would urge us to bring our new natures—our baptized Christian eyes, ears, and hearts—to every part of the Bible. Either this is the Word of God, or it is not. He would have us remember that this is our heavenly Father speaking to us in the Bible and this is how he wants to bless Christian households.

Here is what Paul says: "As the church submits to Christ, so also wives are to submit to their husbands in everything." Here is the point of comparison: With what spirit does the church submit to Christ? Why do we follow his lead? Because Jesus is holding a big stick over our heads? No. It is because Jesus is our Savior who loves us and has our best interests at heart. In that spirit, a Christian wife willingly supports and follows the lead of her husband, not in a servile, slavish manner but with a cheerful, helpful, and informed deference. If this is how Christ designed things and wants things, then that's how she wants it too.

Husbands, contrary to any caricatures, don't get the easy part of this equation.

> **[25]Husbands, love your wives, in the same way as Christ loved the church and gave himself up for her [26]to make her holy, by cleansing her with the washing of water in connection with the Word. [27]He did this so that he could present her to himself as a glorious church, having no stain or wrinkle or any such thing, but so that she would be holy and blameless. [28]In the same way, husbands have an obligation to love their own wives as their own bodies. He who loves his wife loves himself. [29]To be sure, no one has ever hated his own body, but nourishes and cherishes it, just as Christ does the church, [30]because we are members of his body, of his flesh and of his bones.**

"Love my wife? Oh, yes, sure, of course I love her." Is it that easy? Talk is cheap. Love is as love does. Here again is the point of comparison: "Husbands, love your wives, in the same way as Christ loved the church and gave himself up for her"—in the same way as Christ loved us enough to make his death count for ours and made all this our own when he washed us in the gospel waters of Baptism, making the church his beautiful bride, robed in his righteousness. In this way husbands ought to "love their own wives as their own bodies," says Paul. You wouldn't purposely smash your own thumb with a hammer or starve yourself. You don't hate your own body. You feed and care for it, nourish it, and *cherish* it—literally, keep it warm—says Paul. How warm is your love?

How much does Christ love the church? He died for her. Ask just about any man, "Would you be willing to die for your wife?" He might just straighten up like John Wayne and say, "Well, of course! I'd throw myself on a grenade for the little woman. I'd take a bullet for her." Wonderful. Then maybe you wouldn't mind helping her with the dishes or tucking the kids into bed

5:22-33 The Mystery of Christ's Love for Us Inspires Our Own

when she's tired. Then surely you wouldn't think of putting your own interests ahead of hers.

How this mystery of Christ's love for the church inspires our own love goes back to the very beginning. Paul says:

> **³¹"For this reason a man will leave his father and mother and be joined to his wife, and the two will be one flesh." ³²This is a great mystery, but I am talking about Christ and the church. ³³In any case, each one of you also is to love his wife as himself, and each wife is to respect her husband.**

"This is a great mystery," says Paul. Not in some New Age way, not in some way that we can never know, but in a way to which only God can clue us in. Our love for one another can never match the great mystery of Christ's love for us, his church. But the love of Christian husbands and wives can be a silhouette of the love between Christ and his people, this mystery of his great love that he has revealed in the gospel.

So the picture of godly womanhood and Christlike manhood is not something out of the Dark Ages after all. It is something beautiful beyond words if both bear the mark of lives lived with Christ. If we have the eyes of faith, we will see this in the serene face of an older woman sitting day after day at her husband's bedside when he can no longer speak. We will see it in an old man holding the hand of his wife with a tenderness that young sweethearts cannot yet comprehend. We will see it in their crinkly eyes as they look at each other, each one weathered but warmed by the journey.

We who have left our dirty handprints all over the blessing of marriage will find new strength to swim upstream against the tide of our times by trusting him who spilled his blood to wash our dirty hands and hearts. It's like that line in the gospel of Luke:

"When all the people (including the tax collectors) heard this, they declared that God was just [that God was right!]" (7:29). That's it right there! Real repentance is a change of heart and mind. It's when we stop arguing with God, when we stop taking orders from our own sinful selves and from the culture around us, when our hearts are softened enough to say that God is right and we are wrong. It's when we go to the only place where real love can be found: the foot of the cross.

This is how the mystery of Christ's love for us seasons our marriages and becomes a foretaste of the marriage feast yet to come. It is as though Jesus says, "The secret of the Lord is with those who love me. Hang around with me. Sit down next to me. I'm happy to tell you."

6:1-4
The Spirit Turns Our Hearts Toward Home

Despite the chapter division, verses 1-9 continue to speak of the various ways in which being "filled with the Spirit" (5:18) colors our joyful submissiveness in other contexts. You may recall that at the end of the Small Catechism, Martin Luther tacked on what he called the Table of Duties. For husbands and wives, parents and children, pastors and parishioners, laborers and management, he set forth the Bible passages that apply to each, summing it all up with a rhyme: "Let each the lesson learn with care, and all the household well shall fare."

The household of faith, as the Bible refers to it, is just that, a household filled with all kinds of people. Parents and grandparents, children and grandchildren, husbands and wives, single folks and widows, working stiffs and bosses, teachers and students, preachers and parishioners—all serve God at the altars of their various callings. Each person's shop, kitchen, office, or farm is the pulpit from which they let their light shine for Christ.

Here in the closing chapters of his letter to the Christians at Ephesus, Paul outlines this very thing. He previously outlined

EPHESIANS The Unsearchable Riches of Christ

for husbands and wives how their marriages can pick up on the accents of the Savior's love for his church and the church's love for the Savior. Now he urges children and parents to turn their hearts toward home.

In the very last lines of the Old Testament, the prophet Malachi foretells the coming of the great forerunner and the second Elijah, John the Baptist, who would prepare human hearts for the coming of the Christ. "Look! I am going to send Elijah the prophet to you before the great and fearful day of the LORD comes! He will turn the hearts of fathers to their children and the hearts of children to their fathers. Otherwise, I will come and strike the land with complete destruction" (Malachi 4:5-6).

That's it. Then the prophets fall silent. Centuries pass. And when many hearts have grown weary of waiting or have turned elsewhere, the angel Gabriel appears to an old priest named Zechariah as he offers up incense in the Holy Place. Gabriel tells the old man that he and his wife are to become the parents of the great forerunner of the Savior. Borrowing the language of the prophet Malachi, the angel tells Zechariah that this son "will turn many of the sons of Israel back to the Lord their God. He will go before him in the spirit and power of Elijah, to turn the hearts of the fathers to the children, to turn the disobedient to the wisdom of the righteous, to prepare a people who are ready for the Lord" (Luke 1:16-17). Where this does not happen, nothing will be left but a curse upon those unprepared for the coming of Christ.

For those long ago who waited for Christ's first coming or for you and me who await his second coming in the clouds of glory, the road to being ready is always repentance, turning from the sins that bind us and turning toward the Christ who sets us free. This does not start in faraway and exotic places. It begins when the Holy Spirit turns our hearts toward home.

6:1-4 The Spirit Turns Our Hearts Toward Home

Paul says: Children, turn your hearts toward home.

¹Children, obey your parents in the Lord, for this is right. ²"Honor your father and mother," which is the first commandment with a promise: ³"that it may go well with you and that you may live a long life on the earth."

Sometimes we miss the obvious. These letters, these epistles of the New Testament, were read aloud to the congregations to which they were sent. Paul knew this. He says, "Children, obey your parents in the Lord." Paul assumes children will be present in the worship services where his letters are read aloud. He speaks directly to these children. A few lines later, he says, "Fathers, do not provoke your children to anger." He assumes fathers will be sitting in the worship services with their children. He assumes the fathers *bring* their children to church. The fathers do not merely *send* the children. Let us not miss the obvious. Parents and children belong together in God's house. They each get to listen to what God has to say to them as his forgiven children. They each get to listen in on how God wants them to turn their hearts toward home.

Again, sometimes we miss the obvious. "Children, obey your parents *in the Lord*." Paul assumes and implies the children he addresses are baptized little believers. He talks to the Christian nature in each of these little ones and says, "Children, obey your parents"—not because you will be in trouble if you don't, but "obey your parents *in the Lord*." Be what God has made you to be, his own baptized sons and daughters in Christ. Do this because you love the Savior who first loved you and gave himself for you.

Children, turn your hearts toward home. There is no higher service you can do for God in your youth than to obey your parents. Your friendship with Jesus himself is tied up in the way you treat Mom and Dad each day. This means cheerfully doing what your parents ask you to do. This means speaking in a respectful manner to your parents and others in authority. This means consciously trying to mute that attitude in your tone of voice and that "I'm too cool for you" body language. This means looking for ways to honor your parents and guarding the good name they gave you by behaving in a Christian manner. This means appreciating the fact that your parents' endless questions—"Where are you going? . . . When will you be home? . . . What are you going to do? . . . Who will you be with?"—and even their prohibitions—"No, you can't go. . . . No, you can't have that. . . ."—are most often their ways of saying "I love you."

Paul would say, I know this is harder for you as you edge toward adulthood, as you naturally begin to think more independently, as you discover that your parents also have their own failings. Those maddening middle years that our culture calls adolescence leave you conflicted. Are you a child today, or are you a grown-up? Someone has compared this stage of life to the reentry of spaceships returning to earth. If you have ever followed some of these reentries on TV—whether the *Apollo* moonships from years ago or the space shuttles and other space capsules in more recent years—you know there is always a brief blackout in communication. Things heat up during the flaming reentry into the earth's atmosphere, and at that point there is no communication between the spaceship and mission control on earth. Just static. If you have ever watched the movie *Apollo 13*, then you know how everyone breathed a sigh of relief when the voice of an astronaut broke the blackout with something like: "Odyssey here."

6:1-4 The Spirit Turns Our Hearts Toward Home

Something like this may happen between you and your parents during these maddening middle years. You think they don't understand you, even though they were once what you now are. They can't seem to get through to you because you clam up and don't talk to them the way you used to. A certain attitude comes over your face. They ask you to break away from a screen long enough to help out around the house, and you act as though they interrupted a presidential cabinet meeting. You believe that yours is the first generation to have these feelings, that you are far more intelligent than your parents give you credit for, and that your parents sadly have an IQ only slightly above room temperature.

Malachi said that God will "turn . . . the hearts of children to their fathers" (4:6). Children, your hearts turn to your fathers when you give up the attitude and listen to the wisdom of your godly fathers and mothers and grandparents. Children, your hearts turn to your fathers when you stop thinking you are too sophisticated for the words of the Bible. Children, your hearts turn to your fathers when you embrace again the Word and sacraments that your fathers embrace—though they live in a world gone away from God.

God knows you need encouragement to do this, to fight the sinful nature you inherited from your parents and to put up with the unfairness in life that you have come to notice. So, as the foremost command with a promise, the Lord says, "That it may go well with you and that you may live a long life on the earth." You may be quick to notice exceptions that God himself has made to these words of encouragement. But the exceptions prove the rule. Sometimes godly children are snatched away. Sometimes to spare them from things that might have been. Sometimes to call to repentance those who are left behind. Sometimes to remind us that real life—eternal life—always keeps its promise. We cannot get behind the curtain of the hidden God. He is no less loving because of that. *In general*, you *will* have a happier, healthier, longer life if you are not driving drunk, sticking needles in your arms, or sleeping around. You will simply be better off—here and hereafter—if you turn your hearts toward home. And don't worry. In a few years you will notice that, for some reason, your parents seem amazingly smarter.

Parents, you also should turn your hearts toward home:

> **⁴Fathers, do not provoke your children to anger, but bring them up in the training and instruction of the Lord.**

"Fathers" does not exclude moms, but God will not let you dads forget where the buck stops. "Fathers, do not provoke your children to anger"—and therefore make it harder for children to obey—by exasperating them with unreasonable expectations, provoking internal rage with an inconsistent example in your own attitude and actions, making yourself impossible to please, or offering only criticism with little or no encouragement. You exasperate a child if you forget that he or she is still growing and maturing, if you expect a four-year-old to behave like a ten-year-old, if the child exists only to feed your ego on the basketball court or in the classroom.

Fathers, this does not mean abdicating your role as father, as the God-appointed leader in your home. God holds you accountable to exercise this authority with wisdom and understanding, with evenhanded discipline tempered by kindness. There is no love in raising a child to become the tail that wags the dog, the center of his or her own universe, a spoiled brat who will be unbearable to others and eventually to himself or herself.

Fathers and mothers, turn your hearts toward home. You hear horror stories in the news of twisted parents who lock their children in some cellar or cage and starve them. What about parents who fuss over their children's education, sports, dental health, video games, and clothes but keep their immortal souls on a starvation diet, allowing them to walk around spiritually lost yet hoping they will somehow find their way to the Father? This is far worse than dropping them off in the woods somewhere and driving away. It is spiritual child abuse. At stake is where your child will spend eternity. Jesus said, "If anyone causes one of these little ones who believe in me to sin, it would be better for him to have a huge millstone hung around his neck and to be drowned in the depths of the sea" (Matthew 18:6).

Fathers, your hearts turn to your children when you see them as souls for whom Jesus spilled his lifeblood, children who will spend eternity in heaven or hell. Fathers, your hearts turn to your children when you get yourself and your child out of bed and come together with gladness to God's house. This is "the training and instruction of the Lord" that places your child before the mirror of God's law to see how bad off he or she is without Christ and places that child beneath the cross to see how sweet and purified life is with Christ. Fathers, let your children see that a real man is not ashamed to stand up for Jesus. Let them see in their earthly father at least a faint shadow of their heavenly Father.

Long centuries have now passed since the prophet Malachi promised that the coming of the second Elijah would "turn the hearts of fathers to their children and the hearts of children to their fathers" (4:6). John the Baptist came. So did the Savior whose way he prepared. Now we await Christ's final coming. For you children who have failed, Christ became a child for you. He made his obedience yours. For you fathers who have failed, you have a Father in heaven whose compassions are new every morning. There is no better time for all of us—fathers and mothers, sons and daughters, young and old—to turn our hearts toward home.

EPHESIANS

6:5-9
Being Filled With the Spirit Sets Our Hearts Free

In these verses, Paul rounds out his examples of how being "filled with the Spirit" (5:18) inspires a joyful kind of submitting: "Slaves, obey your human masters." As we noted in the previous verses when Paul talks to children and their parents, so here too we dare not miss the obvious. These inspired epistles, or letters, of the New Testament were delivered to various congregations and then read aloud in the church for all to hear. When Paul addresses the children, he assumes they are sitting in the worship service. The same goes for their fathers. So when Paul addresses slaves and then their masters, he assumes that both of these ancient classes of society will be present in the worship services. All rank and privilege slip away when you cross the threshold of God's house.

Slavery was a fact of life in the first century. Neither Christ nor Paul waged a political war against the social institutions of their times. But what a stunning, revolutionary thing among the early Christians that the gospel is the great leveler. Here in the Table of Duties, as the catechism calls it, husbands and wives, parents and children, servants and masters all sit together and discover something breathtakingly beautiful: Our relationship to God is not bound up in our outward circumstances, in the corners where we live out our lives on this earth.

The gospels show us the great Advent preacher, John the Baptist, preparing hearts for the coming of the Savior. In Luke 3:10-14, folks from different walks of life ask John how they can show their repentance. The answers are amazingly simple. If you've got two shirts and someone else has none, give one away. Share your extra sandwich with the one who has none. What about those notorious tax collectors or publicans—Jews who worked for the Roman government? John doesn't tell them to quit their jobs at the revenue office but to be honest tax collectors. He doesn't tell soldiers to quit the military; rather, he exhorts them not to bully people with their power and, of all things, to be content with their wages!

Paul urges us to be content in the corners where God has placed us, like Rudyard Kipling, who could have lived in much fancier places but chose a house by the sea—a house lacking even running water upstairs, indoor bathrooms, and electricity—in a place called Sussex. The old Brit wrote, "God gave all men all earth to love, But since our hearts are small, Ordained for each one spot should prove Beloved over all. . . . Each to his choice, and I rejoice The lot has fallen to me In a fair ground—in a fair ground—Yea, Sussex by the sea!" (Rudyard Kipling, *Sussex*, 1902).

Coming out of a church that exalted holy orders and man-made works, Luther created the Table of Duties, lifted from the epistles of Paul, to emphasize the sacredness of each Christian's vocation, or calling, in life; sacred not because God shouts at us from heaven to be a secretary or a farmer but because all that a Christian does is done for Christ and to Christ.

In his letter to the Corinthians, Paul says, "Each person is to live in the situation the Lord assigned to him—the situation he

6:5-9 Being Filled With the Spirit Sets Our Hearts Free

was in when God called him to faith. I give this same command in all the churches" (1 Corinthians 7:17). That little word *assign* means "to apportion, distribute, deal out." The reality of this life is that not all people will become Oscar nominees, most valuable players, senators, presidents, or Nobel Prize winners. We will not all live in mansions and take home six-figure salaries. So what! These things have nothing to do with our status as sons and daughters of the King of kings. The smallest run-down apartment or the humblest job can become a pulpit for the everlasting gospel.

The gospel of Jesus transforms *us* and our relationships with *one another*. Paul assumes this gospel transformation among Christians in whatever social structure they find themselves.

> **⁵Slaves, obey your human masters with respect and reverence, and with a sincere heart, just as you obey Christ. ⁶Do this not just when they are watching, as if merely to please people, but as slaves of Christ, doing the will of God from the heart. ⁷Serve with eagerness, as for the Lord and not for people, ⁸because you know that each person, whether slave or free, will receive back from the Lord whatever good he has done. ⁹And masters, do the same for your slaves. Do not threaten them, because you know that the one who is both their Master and yours is in heaven, and with him there is no favoritism.**

In the Bible, there are numerous references to slaves and masters, reflecting the reality of that time. The Scriptures do not *promote* slavery. They do not *endorse* slavery. They absolutely do not sanction any submission to earthly masters or authorities *if they command something sinful* (Acts 5:29). Nor do the Scriptures codify any particular form of government or social order.

The Scriptures simply counsel God's people on how to live out their Christian lives in whatever corner of the broken world they happen to live.

It is worth remembering that Paul's letters were meant to be shared and read aloud to the congregations that received them. In addressing masters and slaves in these epistles, it is clear that Paul presumed both would be present in the Christian assemblies. Masters and slaves were on an equal footing and of equal value as redeemed children of God. They were brothers and sisters in Christ. This would influence how they related to each other.

Slavery in any era of history has been attended by cruelty and horrifying injustice. In the very year of Paul's arrival in Rome, a frightful example was recorded by the Roman historian Tacitus. The prefect of the city, Pedanius Secundus, was killed by one of his slaves. In accordance with ancient Roman law, all the slaves belonging to Pedanius (a vast multitude that included women and children) were executed, even though they were innocent of any participation in the crime. The believers of Paul's day were not blind to the evils of chattel slavery, of treating fellow human beings as brute beasts or mere property. In our own country, we fought the Civil War to abolish such injustice and bigotry. American Christians today should not whitewash the historical record of slave trading, cruelty, and lingering racial prejudice and profiling in our own country. Yet the message of Jesus Christ is not a law that can bludgeon people into submission. The sweet gospel message of Jesus' love is meant to melt hard hearts and change stubborn, egotistical minds, which think only of ourselves, into hearts that love our neighbors as ourselves regardless of the amount of melanin in our skin.

Kidnapping and selling a fellow Israelite was a capital offense punishable by death in the Old Testament (Exodus 21:16; Deuteronomy 24:7). In his first letter to Timothy, Paul condemned slave traders alongside murderers and adulterers as "lawless and rebellious people." (See 1 Timothy 1:8-11, where "kidnappers" [EHV] or "menstealers" [KJV] is best understood as a reference to "slave traders" [EHV footnote]). In his first letter to the Corinthians, Paul encouraged slaves to gain their freedom if they could lawfully do so (and there were ways), but if they couldn't, not to worry—they had their real freedom in Christ: hearts set free from sin, guilt, and death by the blood of their Savior, with eternal freedom to come (1 Corinthians 7:20-24).

Under the *civil law* God gave to Moses, the practice of slavery was *regulated*, as were other social realities, such as polygamy and divorce. This was *not* a *moral* stamp of approval. God never approved of or condoned multiple spouses or divorce for any and every reason. The *civil law* simply controlled such things in a less than perfect world. In ancient Israel, people were not warehoused in prisons for minor infractions of civil law, such as damage to property or even theft, but were required to make restitution (sometimes double, sometimes four or five times what was taken). If they were unable to pay, they were compelled to pay back their debt to society by working it off as bondmen (Exodus 22:1,3-4). Seven years was the limit in Hebrew society. And slaves were protected. If a master seriously injured the servant, the servant was set free. Additionally, every 50th year, in the Year of Jubilee, Israelite slaves were to be set free.

Given the choice, who would ever choose bondage over freedom? Yet the Law of Moses provided for just such a possibility (Exodus 21:5-6; Deuteronomy 15:16-17). If a servant found life in his master's house preferable to life as a free laborer elsewhere, he could freely choose to have his ear pierced, to be literally earmarked for his master's service as part of the extended household. That's how it was in ancient Israel.

In Paul's day, among the Gentiles, there were all sorts of servitude. As much as a third of the Roman Empire was made up of slaves or servants of one kind or another. Some were prisoners of war. Some were indentured servants working off their debts. Others were convicts paying for their crimes. Some were born into servitude. Some slaves were actually more educated than their masters. In kinder households, some were considered almost part of the family. Some, though not all, were allowed to acquire property, marry, and eventually buy their freedom (manumission). The Roman orator Cicero wrote that the average length of involuntary servitude was seven years, as it was in Israel. But as a politician, Cicero may have been painting a rosier picture than the reality that existed throughout the Empire.

To the surprise of many people, the apostles did not try to overturn the structures of society by encouraging slaves to disobey or rebel. Immediate abolition of this social order would have thrown the world into chaos. Instead, Paul commanded *Christian* slaves to serve their masters as they'd serve Christ. He commanded *Christian* masters to be fair and just, to remember that they had a Master in heaven to whom they would answer (see Ephesians 6:5-9; Colossians 4:1).

Christianity was certainly a major influence in the gradual, hard-won abolition of slavery in our own country and in other places. The same gospel influence in the hearts of Christians today will move them to promote fairness and justice for all in our own times where racial tensions persist. In many ways this is simply a reflection of the gospel-motivated Golden Rule: "Do for others whatever you want people to do for you" (Matthew 7:12). Or as Abraham Lincoln once said, "As I would not be a slave, so I would not be a master."

6:5-9 Being Filled With the Spirit Sets Our Hearts Free

Freedom in this world is never absolute. Everyone serves someone. Many of the daily "servitudes" in our lives pale in comparison to the horrors of slavery in so many places and in so many chapters of history. Still, it is a fact that if you decide to sleep late and not show up for work, your boss is free to fire you. At various times in history, governments, including our own, have instituted a military draft. Men are compelled to serve whether they want to or not. Those who serve in the military will tell you that they give up many of the daily freedoms we take for granted in order to serve their country. Soldiers are not free to do as they please or live where they please or to disobey orders when it suits them. Life is a thousand and one servitudes. The question is not whether we will spend our lives serving and working, but *for whom* we will do this. Refreshingly, the Bible tells us how to deal with life as it is in a broken world, not with life as we might like it to be.

It is heartwarming to see how the apostles brought the gospel to bear on human relationships, including the relationship between masters and slaves, in a less than perfect world. The influence of Christ's love for us all helped bring about changes for the better where the gospel held sway. May it do the same for the world today.

All this is from the heart of the one Isaiah liked to call the *"servant"* of the Lord (42:1, for example). Jesus said, "The Son of Man did not come to be served, but to *serve*, and to give his life as a ransom for many" (Matthew 20:28). He took "the nature of a *servant*" (Philippians 2:7). He said, "I am among you as one who *serves*" (Luke 22:27). Jesus himself lends a new dignity to the word *servant* as he and his apostles urge us to serve one another in love. In one way or another, it is surely true that we all serve someone in this life. In doing so, we serve Christ.

If you are the master, says Paul, then do not threaten or terrorize your servants, using your position of power to make their lives miserable. Remember that you have a Master in heaven to whom you will one day answer. Your servant is truly free in Christ—and a brother or sister in the faith. As a master, you are set free by Christ to have a servant's heart toward the servant. When you see your servant as one whom Christ loves as much as he loves you, whom Christ thought about when he was dying on the cross just as much as he thought about you, the entire chemistry of your relationship to that person will change.

Christians in positions of power over others in earthly matters nonetheless remember that in Christ there is, as Paul once put it, neither slave nor free, for we are all one in Christ Jesus (Galatians 3:28). The great statesman Daniel Webster understood this. During a summer holiday in a district far away from the Capitol, he went each Sunday to a little country church building. His niece asked him why he went there when he paid little attention to the sermons in Washington. "In Washington," he replied, "they preach to Daniel Webster the statesman. But this man has been talking to Daniel Webster the sinner and telling him of Jesus."

In the Table of Duties, our modern catechisms apply such verses as these to employers and employees—certainly not in the sense that the relationship of a worker to boss is the same as that of slave to master, because the worker is free. Yet, as we see throughout the New Testament, Christians can find applications to such relationships even in a free society. The pendulum between labor and management has swung back and forth since Adam's fall. From Moses to Jeremiah, the prophets thundered against unjust employers holding back the wages of the laboring workers, paying them a pittance and building palaces off the pain of the poor. One can understand why the coal miners felt the need to create a union to stop the widow-making conditions in which they were compelled to labor. But we have seen the

6:5-9 Being Filled With the Spirit Sets Our Hearts Free

pendulum swing in the other direction too—powerful unions protecting incompetent and dangerous employees or purposely fostering mutual mediocrity on the job.

Into the middle of this, the child of God is placed, marching to the beat of a different drummer, whether in labor or management. If you are the worker, then the Bible tells you to do a good job always, not only when the boss is watching you—there are less polite terms for that kind of hypocrisy. As a servant of Christ, with singleness of heart and reverence for the Lord, do your work with all your heart, throwing yourself into your labor, whether pushing a broom or a pencil, knowing that it is the Lord Christ you are serving. If you are the employer—the boss—then remember that you have a Boss in heaven to whom you will one day answer. Being the boss gives you no inherent right to make the lives of your workers miserable with a mean spirit or by unfair treatment.

None of this may sound glamorous, for husbands and wives, parents and children, labor and management. We all have failed a thousand times in these everyday arenas where God has called us to live out our faith before the eyes of a watching world. But for these failures we have the cleansing blood of the one who entered our mundane world to be our Savior. For us, says the Bible, he went to Nazareth as a child and was obedient to his earthly parents. For us, he labored in obscurity in the carpenter's shop. For us, he stretched out those carpenter's hands on a cross to cover our failures and dignify our homeliest duties as acts of worship done to him.

Christ does not call us to abandon our stations in life. Husbands and wives, parents and children, labor and management all have their proper places on this earth. But hearts set free by the blood of him who took upon himself the form of a servant to save us are transformed in how they live out their callings with one another, especially with fellow believers.

The great architect Sir Christopher Wren told a version of this story centuries ago: During the building of the famous St. Paul's Cathedral in London, he came across three workers, each one doing the same hard job, pounding rocks with a sledgehammer. He asked the first man what he was doing. With a snarl, the man said, "I'm breaking rocks!" He asked the second man what he was doing, and the man replied with little enthusiasm: "I'm making a living." He asked the third man what he was doing, and the fellow looked up with a beaming grin and said, "I am building a cathedral!" So it is with hearts set free!

Let each the lesson learn with care, and all the household well shall fare.

EPHESIANS

6:10-17
Put On the Full Armor of God!

The call is to "be strong in the Lord." Of ourselves, we have no strength. But God used Gideon and a mere three hundred men to wipe out the Midianites, who were as numerous as the sand on the seashore. God used the jawbone of a donkey, clutched in the fist of Samson, to break the teeth of his enemies. God used a stick in the hand of Moses to bring an empire to its knees and split the sea, a ruddy-faced shepherd boy from Bethlehem to bring down a walking tank named Goliath, and a one-man army named Elijah to best Jezebel's 450 prophets of Baal. "Be strong in the Lord." A shivering infant in the feed-box of a barn held all the Caesars and Herods of this world in his infant fingers, and one drop of blood from his thorn-pierced brow weighed more than the whole world.

The call to arms here is a summons to be strong in the Lord and in his mighty power and to put on the full armor of God. The words of Ephesians chapter 6 are fighting words. Paul's words sound a militant tone. This is neither popular nor politically correct in many sissified churches today. The fierce doctrinal battles of years gone by and the uncompromising zeal of a John the Baptist or a Martin Luther grate on modern ears. Old hymns such as "Onward, Christian Soldiers" or "Stand Up, Stand Up for Jesus"—with their talk of duty, doctrine, and danger—seem strident, provocative, and alienating. Elsewhere, Paul speaks of waging war with spiritual weaponry, demolishing strongholds, taking thoughts captive, and fighting the good fight. In Revelation chapter 19, the smoke of battle rises from the sacred page. Christ himself, stained with the blood of his defeated foes, is portrayed on a white steed, sounding forth the trumpet that never calls retreat.

> **[10] Finally, be strong in the Lord and in his mighty power. [11] Put on the full armor of God, so that you can stand against the schemes of the Devil. [12] For our struggle is not against flesh and blood, but against the rulers, against the authorities, against the world rulers of this darkness, against the spiritual forces of evil in the heavenly places. [13] For this reason, take up the full armor of God, so that you will be able to take a stand on the evil day and, after you have done everything, to stand.**

"Put on the full armor of God," says Paul, "so that you can stand against the schemes of the Devil." Paul's word for "schemes" is the one from which we get the English word *methods*, as in cunning arts, deceit, craftiness, trickery. The devil has his *methods*.

Paul assumes the existence of the devil, that is, Satan. He says, "Our struggle is not against flesh and blood, but against the rulers, against the authorities, against the world rulers of this darkness, against the spiritual forces of evil in the heavenly places." The "spiritual forces of evil in the heavenly places"

6:10-17 Put On the Full Armor of God!

are above and beyond the physical realm, and so all the more dangerous.

The Bible gets no further than the third chapter of its first book before we meet the old foe in serpent's form, hissing his lethal doubts into the heart of Eve. By verse 15 of that chapter, the battle is joined. Christ and Satan both draw their swords as a promise rises from the ancient page: A hero born of woman will crush the serpent with his heel.

The book of Job portrays the calamities of that ancient sufferer in terms of Satan making his bid for Job's very soul. On the threshold of the New Testament, Christ and Satan become locked in deadly embrace during the wilderness temptations. On the pages of the four gospels, eerie cases of demon possession stalk the Savior's path. The gospels clearly distinguish between the illnesses that Jesus cured and the demons that Jesus drove out. Without embarrassment, St. Luke tells of the disciples returning from their missionary circuit, rejoicing that even the demons bowed low before the name of Christ. Jesus saw this as a great victory in the spiritual realm: "I was watching Satan fall like lightning from heaven," he said (Luke 10:18). And setting aside all cheap psychoanalysis of Judas, the Bible tells us that Satan entered into the traitor.

Peter says, "Have sound judgment. Be alert. Your adversary, the Devil, prowls around like a roaring lion, looking for someone to devour" (1 Peter 5:8). As basic Bible doctrine, the apostle John says in his first epistle, "This is why the Son of God appeared: to destroy the works of the Devil" (1 John 3:8). Unblushingly, the last book of the Bible describes Satan's defeat: "The great dragon was thrown down—the ancient serpent, the one called the Devil and Satan, the one who leads the whole inhabited earth astray" (Revelation 12:9).

A macabre chill confronts us in our so-called post-Christian age: "Is all of this real?" If the powers of darkness are not real, then who needs a Savior? Who needs the cross? Who needs Christ or the Bible or missionaries or Christian schools? If we live out our lives in a closed system where random chance and material cause and effect hold sway, then Satan is just a painted boogeyman concocted to scare little kids into behaving—and Jesus Christ, if he came at all, came for no good reason . . . and died for even less.

"For this reason," says Paul, "take up the full armor of God, so that you will be able to take a stand on the evil day and, after you have done everything, to stand." Now, armor is not something within a person, like strength, wisdom, or courage. Armor is something outside a person that is put on. Listen to how Paul describes it:

> [14]**Stand, then, with the belt of truth buckled around your waist, with the breastplate of righteousness fastened in place,** [15]**and with the readiness that comes from the gospel of peace tied to your feet like sandals.** [16]**At all times hold up the shield of faith, with which you will be able to extinguish all the flaming arrows of the Evil One.** [17]**Also take the helmet of salvation and the sword of the Spirit, which is the word of God.**

"Stand, then, with the belt of truth buckled around your waist." The Roman soldier wore a heavy belt that guarded and supported his middle. It was more than some decorative Elvis belt. It allowed him to tuck in or gird up any loose-flowing robes or clothing in order to be prepared for action, free from anything that would trip him up, free to fight. The Christian's belt is truth. This objective truth is the opposite of the devil's lies. Satan wants you to believe that there is no truth, that nobody can know the truth, that to claim to have the truth is the height of arrogance, and that to be in a state of moral confusion and doctrinal doubt is a sign of pious humility and stupendous intelligence.

In the early centuries of the church, men came together from different countries to set forth the truth plainly and clearly. They did this because heretics—false teachers—had sowed confusion. On the basis of the Bible, these men met in order to clarify "this is true and this is false." They defined heresy, condemned it, and excommunicated the men who taught it. Humanly speaking, if they had not done so, there would be no church today. The results of these early councils were the Apostles', Nicene, and Athanasian creeds. By these creeds, the orthodox leaders of the church said to their people, "This is the substance of your faith according to the Bible. Recite each creed. Get it into your head and heart. Wrap it around you and buckle it on." In similar fashion, we buckled on the belt of truth at the time of the Reformation with the Lutheran Confessions.

So the stammering youngster stands at the teacher's desk and recites, "The wages of sin is death, but the undeserved gift of God is eternal life in Christ Jesus our Lord" (Romans 6:23) and "I believe that I cannot by my own thinking or choosing . . ." (Luther's Explanation to the Third Article) and "Chief of sinners though I be, Jesus shed his blood for me" (CW 578). The youngster is buckling on the belt of God's truth. "I have hidden your sayings in my heart, so that I may not sin against you," says the psalmist (Psalm 119:11). Do we ourselves buckle on the belt of truth in regular Bible reading?

Next, "stand, then, . . . with the breastplate of righteousness fastened in place." The breastplate covered the soldier from the base of the neck to his thighs—in other words, it covered the vital organs. Christ's righteousness covers our innermost beings: the heart, mind, and conscience. These are the sensitive areas where Satan can get at us with the slings and arrows of an evil conscience. Here, within each of us, he injects the failures of a lifetime.

Satan hits our vitals, telling us, as Benjamin Disraeli observed, "Youth is a blunder, manhood a struggle, old age a regret." The years evaporate, and we learn that we are finite. We cannot take back the stupidity of yesterday. We do not have the strength to make today or tomorrow much better.

What is the answer to all this disappointment? Is it not to take up the breastplate of Christ's righteousness each day? Is it not to wrap around yourself this righteousness of another, which infinitely surpasses all the self-help fads offered by the world? Instead of "Look what I have done," wrap around yourself this battle cry: "Look what Christ has done!" This is the breastplate of righteousness.

The next piece of armor may be called the combat boots of the gospel or, as Paul puts it, "the readiness that comes from the gospel of peace tied to your feet like sandals." What better preparedness or readiness is there than to possess the good news of Jesus? Whatever countless therapies may be offered to calm our troubled hearts, the Prince of Peace, the Wonderful Counselor with his gospel, knows how, as Shakespeare once put it, to minister to minds diseased and pluck from the memory rooted sorrows (*Macbeth*, Act V, Scene 3). Or, as Isaiah said it far better, the gospel knows how "to bind up the brokenhearted" (Isaiah 61:1), offering the peace Jesus spoke of, which the world cannot give (John 14:27).

Then there is "the shield of faith," literally, "the shield of *the* faith." Our faith is worthless apart from its content. We do not have faith in faith, but faith in *the faith*—in Christ and all that Christ says. So, says Paul, "Hold up the shield of [the] faith, with

6:10-17 Put On the Full Armor of God!

which you will be able to extinguish all the flaming arrows of the Evil One." This is an easy picture to understand if you've ever watched an old Western. All it takes is one flaming arrow shot into a house or wagon train to start a destructive fire. The devil shoots his arrows to set the houses of our lives on fire—perhaps flaming influences of obscene entertainment on the glowing box, perhaps pointed darts of popular opinion and peer pressure, perhaps paralyzing missiles of intellectual doubts, or perhaps burning arrows of discouragement.

Against all these, we need a shield. My brain isn't a shield against Satan's attacks. For all my attempts to figure out the answer to the question *why*, I discover that better heads than mine have been smashed to pieces on the rocks of life's hard questions. Science is not a shield. Today's science is tomorrow's foolishness. One day chocolate and coffee will kill me, but the next day they are wonder drugs. What seems like sure scientific proof for the Bible is debunked by the next discovery. My denominational membership is not a shield. "Orthodox" people can go to hell too. What I need is *the* faith—that which was believed by Noah, the preacher of righteousness; by Abraham, the friend of God; by the centurion and the Syrophoenician woman; by the heroes of Hebrews chapter 11. That which shielded them still shields me, both the content—"the faith"—and the Spirit-wrought faith that lays hold of that content.

And, says Paul, "take the helmet of salvation." There is nothing quite so lethal as a head injury. The devil goes for the head, for the fatal blow, to rob us of our salvation in Christ.

Salvation is a rich word in the Bible. When an Israelite heard the word *salvation*, he or she thought of how God rescued his people at the Red Sea when seemingly there was no way out. "Stand firm, and see the salvation from the Lord," said Moses (Exodus 14:13). God arms us with the helmet of salvation, the deliverance wrought by another who went for the head of the enemy: Christ is the hero born of woman who crushed the head of the serpent with his heel (Genesis 3:15). "You are to give him the name Jesus, because he will save his people from their sins" (Matthew 1:21). Only Jesus can ward off the enemy's attacks on our defenseless heads. Thus the old hymn verse: "Myself I cannot save, myself I cannot keep; but strength in Thee I surely have, whose eyelids never sleep" (*The Lutheran Hymnal* 433:5).

And so we come to the one offensive weapon in God's arsenal: "the sword of the Spirit, which is the word of God." As Jesus wielded the sword of the Spirit with specific utterances of God in the wilderness, saying to Satan, "It is written," so this is a sword that must be taken from the scabbard and used. It will do little good to beat our chests like apes, shouting, "We have the Word in its truth and purity," if we leave the Bible on the shelf.

We may be tempted to use other weapons, but the book of Hebrews reminds us, "The word of God is living and active, sharper than any double-edged sword" (Hebrews 4:12). This double-edged sword of God's Word—correctly handled and rightly divided into law and gospel (2 Timothy 2:15)—is the one offensive weapon that Christ used against the dark powers, saying, "It is written!" Christ expects us to use it too.

"Take up the full armor of God, so that you will be able to take a stand on the evil day and, after you have done everything, to stand," says the great apostle. "The evil day" comes for each of us. Job had his day. Joseph in Pharaoh's dungeon had his. David in the badlands of Judea had his. You and I will have ours. Now is the day and now is the hour to put on the full armor of God.

EPHESIANS

6:18-24
Pray!

With a chain dangling from his wrist, Paul penned the final lines of his letter to the Christians at Ephesus. While under the watchful eye of the Roman guard, Paul packed a lot into these six chapters. Throughout the book he points us to God's plan to save us before time was. He paints for us a picture of how God carried out this plan in time through Jesus Christ, whose doing and dying and rising in our stead comes into our feeble hands and hearts by grace alone, by a God-given faith in Christ alone. He tells us how God has gathered all of us who trust in Christ into one body, the holy Christian church. He takes our eyes off the hard road here in the wilderness and fixes our gaze on the glories to come.

But the apostle who had one foot in heaven still had one foot on earth. In Ephesians he teaches us about the ministry and about the relentless civil war between our sinful nature and our Christian nature. He applies the law and gospel to our sexual sins, our tempers, our greed, our drinking habits, and our foul mouths. He holds in front of us what Luther called in his catechism the Table of Duties—the separate callings by which we honor God in our lives as husbands and wives, parents and children, labor and management. And to fight the good fight through to the end, Paul bids us to put on the full armor of God: the belt of truth, the breastplate of righteousness, the combat boots of the gospel's peace, the shield of faith, the helmet of salvation, and the sword of the Spirit that is the Word of God.

But there is one more summons. Paul references prayer four times. A hymn says, "Put on the gospel armor, each piece put on with *prayer*" (CW 872). We know that none of this is mechanical. Clearly, a knowledge of the Bible and its teachings is crucial. You cannot believe what you do not know. But neither is all this just an intellectual exercise. A man may recite Psalm 23 with all the skill of a Shakespearean actor, "The Lord is my shepherd . . . ," but if he believes none of it, he goes to hell. Another man may stumble as he says the same words, but those words hold him up when he crosses the dark valley and go with him to the Father's home. What's the difference? One man knows Psalm 23. The other man knows the Good Shepherd.

Faith implies a relationship between God and his children. The fruit of any relationship is communication. Husbands and wives, parents and children, people in general who care about one another—they communicate; they talk. It's as natural as water being wet. So it is with our relationship to our Father in heaven: He talks to us. We talk to him. We dare never confuse the two. God talks to us on the pages of the Bible. We talk to God in prayer.

Our prayers are not the North Star on our journey home. Too many hearts, charging down some wrong road, wrap a phony piety around their self-will by saying, "I have prayed about this, and God wants me to be happy. I think God wants me to . . ." Here you may fill in the blank: "Find a nicer spouse; move in with my boyfriend; compromise the scriptural teachings I once vowed to uphold; etc." God has already told you what he wants . . . in 66 books of the Bible. This is where God talks to you. In prayer you talk to God, agree with God, thank God, and ask God. If the conversation is only one way—a self-willed whining to God where we do all the talking, where God can't get a word in edgewise, where we excuse our habitual avoidance of God's house with "Well, I don't go to church, but I pray all the time," where there is no desire to hear the preaching of the Word, to partake of the sacrament, to search the Scriptures—then the conversation dries up. Communication breaks down. So does the relationship.

None of this belittles prayer. It puts it in its proper order. Once God has spoken, it will not do to give our Father the silent treatment, to say nothing in response. A Christian who does not pray is like a lung that does not breathe and a heart that does not beat. In short, that Christian is dead.

Four times in these closing lines of Ephesians, Paul bids us to pray:

> **[18]At every opportunity, pray in the Spirit with every kind of prayer and petition. Stay alert for the same reason, always persevering in your intercession for all the saints. [19]Pray for me also, that when I open my mouth a message will be given to me that boldly reveals the mystery of the gospel, [20]for which I am an ambassador in chains. Pray that I may speak about it boldly, as it is necessary for me to speak.**

From the time our godly fathers and mothers folded our hands and prayed with us before tucking us in at night, our sinful flesh has haunted our hearts with doubts. Is God really

EPHESIANS The Unsearchable Riches of Christ

there? Does Jesus really listen? Does he really answer? Is he able and willing to help?

Harry Emerson Fosdick was one of the most famous preachers of liberal Protestantism in the United States in the first half of the 20th century. He said in one of his books that it is heathenish to pray for rain. He said that if it rains tomorrow, it will not be because anybody said some prayers today but because the sun shone on the Indian Ocean six weeks ago. And if it is supposed to rain tomorrow, it will rain whether anyone prays or not. And if no rain is on the schedule, then it will not rain no matter how many people pray. That's what Harry Emerson Fosdick said.

But he's dead. And Christ lives. And God tells us in the Bible that "the prayer of a righteous person is able to do much because it is effective," and then adds, "Elijah was a man just like us. He prayed earnestly that it would not rain, and it did not rain on the land for three years and six months. Then he prayed again, and the sky gave rain, and the land produced its harvest" (James 5:16-18). So, clearly, it is Harry Emerson Fosdick who is the heathen. As Tennyson put it, "More things are wrought by prayer than this world dreams of" (*Idylls of the King*).

Paul bids the Ephesian Christians and us to pray because the Bible says that God rules and governs the world through the prayers of his people. In ways beyond our understanding, both before and after events, God takes into account the prayers of his people. It is for the sake of God's elect that the world continues to exist at all. It was Jesus himself who taught us to pray and who promised to hear us.

So again, four times Paul bids us to pray. Though it may not seem as evident in our English translation, in the precise Greek language in which Paul wrote, he also uses the word *all* four times—bidding us to pray "at *every* opportunity," "with *every* kind of prayer and petition," "*always* persevering in your intercession for *all* the saints"—that is, believers in Christ.

Consider each one of these. "At every opportunity, pray in the Spirit with every kind of prayer and petition." To pray "in the Spirit" means that the Holy Spirit prompts us to pray, creating in us a longing for conversation with our Father. "At every opportunity" doesn't imply there is something wrong with our table prayers and bedtime prayers. It is a sad thing if these are not practiced in Christian homes. But "at every opportunity" means more, to begin the day with prayer before urgently rushing off to the rat race or to silence the screens long enough to have a brief devotion with the family. A Scripture lesson and prayer, a hymn verse, a few lines from the catechism, a page out of the *Meditations* booklet in the napkin holder, a Bible story before bedtime—these are some of the opportunities Paul has in mind. "At every opportunity" means talking to God, silently or aloud, formally or informally, throughout the ups and downs of our day—when the sun is shining and when the clouds roll in, when life tastes sweet and when the hours turn bitter, when we see others struggling and when we see doors opening for the gospel. Christ is not our fire extinguisher. He is our friend and companion on all occasions.

Pray "with every kind of prayer and petition," says Paul. Christian scholars have divided prayer into all kinds of categories. Really, there are two basic types—the ones in which we ask God for something and the ones in which we thank God for something. We all nod our heads in embarrassment each time we hear the story of the ten lepers who all *asked* Jesus to heal them, and he did, but only one came back to *thank* Jesus.

We do not have to look far for a reason to pray with thankful hearts throughout the day: for our baptism into Christ's family, for the banquet of Word and sacrament spread before us, for the love of family and friends, for food and shelter, for the health to get up each day, both when we are sick and all the days when we are not sick. The list is endless. So are the requests. Our Father is not tired of listening. He will not say, "Oh, it's you again! Now what do you want?!" Over and over, Christ opens his arms and says, "Come to me. Tell me all about it. Cast your burdens and worries on me. I delight to listen. I want to help. I can. I will. You can talk to me about that painful memory, about yesterday's sin and guilt. That's why I came down from heaven in the first place. You can talk to me about your troubled home, your wayward son or daughter, your upcoming operation, your job and your groceries, your loneliness and your fear of dying, your disappointments, and your failures. And as you talk to me, open your heart also to what I have to say to you in my Word, in my promises, in my guidance."

And, says Paul, "Stay alert for the same reason, always persevering in your intercession for all the saints." Luke introduces our Lord's parable of the persistent widow by saying that "Jesus told [his disciples] a parable about the need to always pray and not lose heart" (Luke 18:1). It is a hard thing to wait for God, to persevere and set your hopes on what you thought must surely be the will of God for your life only to find that God had other plans. Perhaps you banged on God's door for a recovery from some illness, for the birth of a healthy child, for a promotion or at least some appreciation at the shop, for a stubborn child to turn around before it's too late. Perhaps things turned out badly . . . or at least differently from what you had prayed. You sat there wondering: Does it pay to pray? Why does God delay? Will Jesus ever come down that road to help me? But pray with all perseverance anyway. Don't lose heart! Isaac, seemingly destined for death, came dancing down that mountain with old Abraham. And Joseph walked from the dungeon to the throne in a single day. And Jesus . . . well . . . Jesus turned Good Friday into Easter Sunday.

And we should not limit our prayers to ourselves, says Paul: "Persevering in your intercession for all the saints." All who believe in Christ are saints, people set apart by faith in Christ, people inside the circle with Christ. They all need our prayers too—the missionaries in far-off places, that they and theirs may be kept safe and that the gospel may take root; our fellow Christians elsewhere, that they may not fall prey to poisonous false teachings; our country in its descent into a moral graveyard; the sick and the poor; teachers and pastors—*all* the saints. After all, you're always a bit happier when you are not thinking about yourself so much, aren't you?

And speaking of pastors, Paul is not afraid to ask the Ephesians to pray for *him* as he bids them farewell:

21Tychicus, our dear brother and a faithful minister in the Lord, will tell you everything, so that you also may know how I am and what I am doing. 22I am sending him to you for this very reason, that you may know how we are, and that he may comfort your hearts. 23Peace to the brothers, and love with faith from God the Father and the Lord Jesus Christ. 24Grace be with all who have an undying love for our Lord Jesus Christ. Amen.

Like all preachers of the gospel, Paul craves the prayers of God's people to hold up his prophet hands in the great battle— that being tired *in* the work, he may not become tired *of* the work; that being opposed by the world, he may never be ashamed of the gospel; that discouragement may never become cowardice; that words may be given to him to fearlessly make known the mystery of the gospel for which he is now in chains. So, from afar, the great lion of God raises his hands in blessing over them and over us, bidding us to pray as we love our Lord Jesus Christ with an undying love.

To God be glory now and forever for all the unsearchable riches of Christ!

Soli Deo Gloria